TESTING OF MATERIALS

DR S JEYASUDHA | DR R SURESH | DR R SANJEEV KUMAR | B V SAI THRINATH AND DR A RAJKUMAR

Made with ♥ on the Notion Press Platform
www.notionpress.com

THIS BOOK IS DEDICATED TO LORD SHIRDI SAI BABA AND MY MOTHER P.BALANAGAMMAL

Contents

Foreword

Materials for electrcal and mechanical engineering are very much important for further development of machinery things and equipments. these materials are tested by using different methods and folloed some standards also. without testing of all meterials we cannot develop or create the machines and equipment.

This book is aimed at the graduate level students or engineer mainly interested in material handling and is indeded to provide some practical reference. This book is organized so that it can be used as a text book. This book has been written mainly for those who have teken a corse of Testing of Materials. However enough introductory material has been included to make the readable even by motivated readers whose only knowledge of mechanical and electrical elements.

This material covered with five chapters which are summerised below,

1. INTRODUCTION TO MATERIALS TESTING
2. MECHANICAL TESTING
3. NON DESTRUCTIVE TESTING
4. MATERIAL CHARACTERIZATION TESTING
5. OTHER TESTING

This book is well structured and defined to provide the necessary information for the material testing.

Preface

This book TESTING OF MATERIALS has been written to provide adequate knowledge on destructive, non destructive metials, nano materials and testing. It is designed as a text for UG level course in Electrical and Mechanical Branch in the professional colleges affiliated to universities in India. The purpose of this book is to present an introductory level of testing of the materials.

The materials available with the listed reference books have a significant impact on this book. I am greatefully indebted to the authors and publishers of this book and the reference books.

Acknowledgements

My wholehearted and sincere thanks to the "ALMIGHTY" for enabling me to do my task successfully.

This Book was carried out in the Department of Electrical and Electronics Engineering, K.Ramakrishnan College of Engineering, Trichy. Numerous souls have given a lot of encouragement during this work directly or indirectly contributed to its success. It is my privilege to express my gratitude to all of them.

Most of all, I would like to express my sincere gratitude to my Brother Mr.S.GOKUL PRAN, Assistant Professor, CSE Department, Sri Vidhya Nikethan Engineering College, Tirupati, for his direction and support.

I gratefully acknowledge, Dr.R.Suresh, Assistant Professor in the Department of Mechanical Engineering, Christian College of Engineering and Technology, Dindigul, Tamilnadu, Dr. R. Sanjeev Kumar, Professor, Department of Mechanical Engineering, Swarnandhra College of Engineering and Technology, Narasapur, Andhra Pradesh, Mr.B.V.Sai Thrinath, Assistant Professor in the EEE Department, Mohan Babu University,(Formerly Sree Vidyanikethan Engineering College), Tirupati, Andhrapradesh and Dr.A.Rajkumar Professor and Head, Department of EEE, K.Ramakrishnan College of Technology, Trichy, for their valuable help and suggestions.

I would like to thank Mr.M.Dhayaanithi and Mr.R.Surya Department of EEE, K.Ramakrishnan College of Technology, Trichy for their help to edit this book.

Finally, I would like to express my deepest gratitude to my father, my mother Mrs. P. Balanagammal and my husband Dr. S. Gandhi for their endless support, my brothers Mr. S. Muruganantham (late) and Mr. S. Muralikumar for their support, advice and encouragement. My thanks are due to all my family members and kind-hearted souls who directly or indirectly contributed to the progress of this book.

Syllabus

TESTING OF MATERIALS

OBJECTIVE:

To understand the various destructive and non destructive testing methods of materials and its industrial applications.

CHAPTER I INTRODUCTION TO MATERIALS TESTING

Overview of materials, Classification of material testing, Purpose of testing, Selection of material, Development of testing, Testing organizations and its committee, Testing standards, Result Analysis, Advantages of testing.

CHAPTER II MECHANICAL TESTING

Introduction to mechanical testing, Hardness test (Vickers, Brinell, Rockwell), Tensile test, Impact test (Izod, Charpy) - Principles, Techniques, Methods, Advantages and Limitations, Applications. Bend test, Shear test, Creep and Fatigue test - Principles, Techniques, Methods, Advantages and Limitations, Applications.

CHAPTER III NON DESTRUCTIVE TESTING

Visual inspection, Liquid penetrate test, Magnetic particle test, Thermography test – Principles, Techniques, Advantages and Limitations, Applications. Radiographic test, Eddy current test, Ultrasonic test, Acoustic emission-Principles, Techniques, Methods, Advantages and Limitations, Applications.

CHAPTER IV MATERIAL CHARACTERIZATION TESTING

Macroscopic and Microscopic observations, Optical and Electron microscopy (SEM and TEM) - Principles, Types, Advantages and Limitations, Applications. Diffraction techniques, Spectroscopic Techniques, Electrical and Magnetic Techniques- Principles, Types, Advantages and Limitations, Applications.

CHAPTER V OTHER TESTING

Thermal Testing: Differential scanning calorimetry, Differential thermal analysis. Thermo-mechanical and Dynamic mechanical analysis: Principles, Advantages, Applications. Chemical Testing: X-Ray Fluorescence

OUTCOME

1. Identify suitable testing technique to inspect industrial component www.rejinpaul.com downloaded from.
2. Ability to use the different technique and know its applications and limitations

ONE

INTRODUCTION TO MATERIALS TESTING

1.1 Overview of materials

Materials testing is a well-established technique used to determine the physical and mechanical properties of raw materials and components from a human hair to steel, composite materials and ceramics.

To meet the challenges posed in testing a wide diversity of materials AMETEK Test & Calibration Instruments offers a comprehensive range of high performance materials testing machines, designed to make accurate and repeatable force measurements in the range from 0.1 N to 300 kN (0.0225 lbf - 67443 lbf). Depending on the machine, elongations of between 1 micron and 2.5 m (98.4 in) can be measured.

What is Material Science and Engineering ?

Processing → Structure → Properties → Performance

Understanding of the relationship among structure, properties, processing, and performance of materials.

Defenition : Material science is the investigation of the relationship among processing, structure, properties, and performance of materials.

Historical Perspective

- Beginning of the Material Science - People began to make tools from stone – Start of the **Stone** Age about two million years ago. Natural materials: stone, wood, clay, skins, etc.
- The Stone Age ended about 5000 years ago with introduction of **Bronze** in the Far East.
- The **Iron** Age began about 3000 years ago and continues today.

Age of Advanced materials: throughout the Iron Age many new types of materials have been introduced (**ceramic, semiconductors, polymers, composites...).**

- Example is the dramatic progress in the strength to density ratio of materials, that resulted in a wide variety of new products, from dental materials to tennis racquets

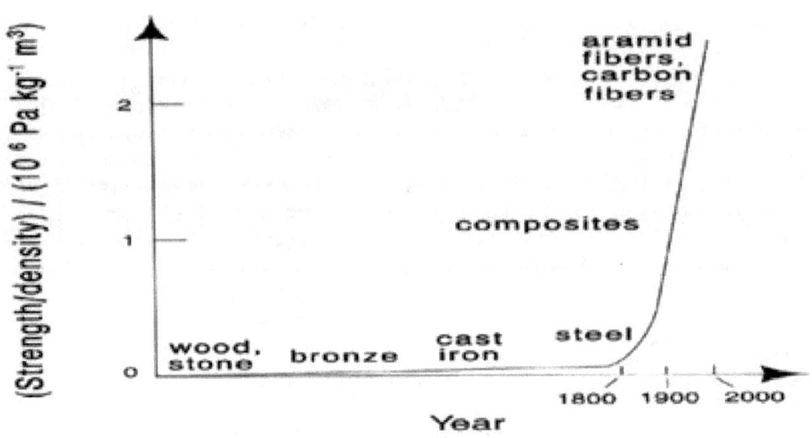

Fig. 1 Material strength/Density ratio for year

Typical testing capabilities include:

- Tensile Strength
- Compression
- Flexure / Bend Strength
- Coefficient of Friction
- Puncture Strength
- Tear Resistance
- Peel Strength
- Shear Strength
- Delamination Strength
- Bond Strength
- Adhesion Strength
- Break Load
- Creep and Stress Relaxation
- Crush Resistance
- Deformation Strength
- Ductility
- Elastic Limit
- Elongation
- Rupture Strength
- Young's Modulus
- Toughness

Applications of Material Testing Machines

Materials testing machines are suitable for use in quality control, production, laboratory, R&D or education. The extensive testing capabilities listed above mean that there is a diverse range of applications in markets such as:

- Plastics
- Rubber
- Packaging
- Automotive
- Medical
- Pharmaceutical

- Metals
- Paper and Board
- Wood
- Textiles
- Electronics Building Materials

Basic classifications of Materials

According to Budinski : materials may be classified as shown below:

1) Metals and alloys.

2) Ceramics.

3) Polymers.

4) Composites.

5) Advanced materials: such as semiconductors, biomaterials, smart materials, and nano engineered materials.

1.Metals: Metals are elements which have free valence electrons which is responsible for electricity. Metallic bond of the metal is electrostatic force . Eg. Cu, Fe, Zn, Ag,

Alloys**:** Metallic materials formed by mixing two or more elements such as Mils steel (Fe+C), Stainless steel (FE+C+Cr+Mn....etc)

Properties

High electrical conductivity.

High thermal conductivity.

Ductile and relatively high stiffness.

Toughness and strength.

Applications

Structures

Automobiles

Airplanes

Trains

Machine tools

2.Ceramics: Inorganic, non-metallic crystalline compounds and are bound by Coulomb forces. They are usually combinations of metals or semiconductors with oxygen, nitrogen or carbon (oxides, nitrides, and carbides). SiO_2,SiC,Si_3N_4

Properties

Light weight, Hard.

High strength.

Tend to be brittle.

Low electrical conductivity.

High temperature resistance.

Corrosion resistance.

Applications

Electrical insulators

Thermal insulation Windows, television screens, optical fibers glass

Corrosion resistant

Magnetic materials

3.Polymers:It is long chain molecule made up of many repeating units, called **monomers.** Polymers can be natural (organic) or synthetic. They are bound by covalent forces and also by weak van der Waals forces. Eg. Plastics, cosmetics, rubbers, etc.

Properties

Compared with metals:

1. Polymers have lower density lower stiffness and tend to creep.
2. High thermal expansion and corrosion resistance.
3. Low electrical and thermal conductivities.
4. Not withstand high temperatures.

Applications

1. Adhesives and glues
2. Containers
3. Moldable products
4. Clothing material
5. Biomaterials
6. Liquid crystals
7. Synthetic oils and greases

4. *Composite:* A combination of two or more materials to achieve better properties than that of the original materials. The primary objective of engineering composites is to increase **strength to weight ratio**. Eg. Cement, Thick steel fibers

Properties

1. Low weight
2. High stiffness.
3. Brittle.
4. Low thermal conductivity.
5. High fatigue resistance.

Applications

1.Sports equipment (golf shafts, tennis rackets, bicycle frames)
2.Aerospace materials
3.Thermal insulation
4.Concrete
5."Smart" materials (sensing and responding)
6.Brake materials

5. *Advanced Materials:*

- Materials that are utilized in high-technology applications are sometimes termed *advanced materials.*
- Examples include electronic equipment (camcorders, CD/DVD players, etc.), computers, fiber-optic systems, spacecraft, aircraft, and military rocketry.
- These advanced materials are typically traditional materials whose **properties have been enhanced**, and also newly developed, high-performance materials.

It includes ***Semiconductors, Biomaterials, Smart materials, Nanomaterials***

a. Semiconductors:

- Semiconductors have **electrical properties** that are intermediate **between** the electrical **conductors** (i.e., metals and metal alloys) and **insulators** (i.e., ceramics and polymers).
- The **electrical characteristics** of these materials are extremely **sensitive** to the presence of minute concentrations of impurity atoms, for which the concentrations may be controlled over very small spatial regions.
- Semiconductors have made possible the **advent of integrated circuitry** that has totally revolutionized the electronics and computer industries over the past three decades.

b. **Biomaterials :**

- Biomaterials are employed in components implanted into the human body to replace diseased or damaged body parts. stem
- These materials must not produce toxic substances and must be compatible with body tissues (i.e., must not cause adverse biological reactions).
- All of the preceding materials (metals, ceramics, polymers, composites, and semiconductors) may be used as biomaterials.
- Eg. contact lenses, pacemakers, heart valves, orthopedic devices, etc..

c. Smart Materials :

- Smart (or intelligent) materials are a group of new and state-of-the-art materials and developed for many of our technologies.
- These materials are able to sense changes in their environment and then respond to these changes in predetermined
- The "smart" concept is being extended to rather sophisticated systems that consist of both smart and traditional materials
- Components of a smart material (or system) include some type of **sensor** (that detects an input signal), and an **actuator** (that performs a responsive and adaptive function).
- Actuators may be called upon to change shape, position, natural frequency, or mechanical characteristics in response to changes in temperature, electric fields, and/or magnetic fields.

d. Nano materials

- Nano materials are defined as engineered materials with a least one dimension in the range of 1-100 nm. (equivalent to approximately 500 atom diameters).
- Particles of "***nano***" size have been shown to exhibit enhanced or novel properties including **reactivity**, **greater sensing** capability and **increased mechanical strength.**
- The nano technique offers simple, clean, fast, efficient, and economic for the synthesis of a variety of organic molecules, to **switch from traditional method.**
- Nano materials may be any one of the four basic types: metals, ceramics, polymers, and composites. However, unlike these other materials, they are not distinguished on the basis of their chemistry, but rather, size;
- Prior to the advent of nano materials, the chemistry and physics of materials was to begin by studying **large and complex structures.**
- Then to investigate the fundamental building blocks of these structures that are **smaller and simpler**. This approach is sometimes termed "top-down" science.
- The development of scanning probe **microscopes** permits **observation** of individual **atoms and molecules**
- This ability to carefully **arrange atoms** provides opportunities to **develop** mechanical, electrical, magnetic, and other **properties.**
- We call this the "bottom-up" approach, and the study of the properties of these materials is termed *nanotechnology*.

Classification of Nano material

All conventional materials like metals, semiconductors, glass, ceramic or polymers can in principle be obtained with a nano-scale dimension. The classification of nano materials can follow different criteria like the size, the phase composition and the way of manufacturing

Nanoscale in three dimensions: such as

- *Nanoparticles*: are often defined as particles of less than 100 nm in diameter. Nanoparticles are formed by tens or hundreds of atoms and can have different size and shape.
- *Fullerenes*: Spherical molecule formed of hexagonal carbon structure (carbon atoms forming a "ball" of nanometer diameter).

Fig. 2. **Nanomaterials in three dimensions**

Nanomaterials in two dimensions

- Two dimensional nano materials such as tubes (carbon nanotubes -CNT) and wires.
- Carbon nanotubes: are linear structures that can reach microns of length with nano metric diameter. They can be single or multiwall.

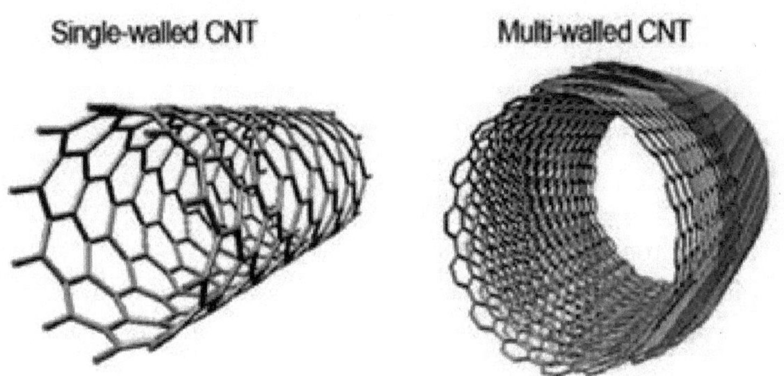

Fig. 3 Three Dimentional Nanoparticle

Nanomaterial in one dimension

In this category belong nano materials such as **thin films** and **engineered surfaces**, such as grapheme and inorganic layer.

Graphene: is formed by a layer of a carbon atoms, while other inorganic layers can be grown to modify the surfaces of bulk materials.

Fig. 4 Nano in one dimentional

Nanolayers: are a very important class of nanomaterials. Often they are used to **modify the surface of bulk materials.**

Nanomaterials classification according to phase composition criterion:

- In the **nano composites** (phase composition criterion) materials a nanomaterial (nanoparticles, nanotubes, layers) acts as a filler of a matrix material that in most cases is a polymer.
- *Inorganic nanoparticles* (red spots) are mixed with the **polymeric matrix** (Blue). The nano material contribute to the nano composites new or **improved properties** (mechanical, electrical, optical etc.)

Snapshot of polymer nanocomposites

Fig. 5 Nano Composition - Polymer

In the nanocomposites the material matrix can be different from a polymer. Another common **matrix** is the **ceramic** or the glass (inorganic nano-composites): the glass is mixed with nanoparticles to obtain different colors.

Fig. 6. Nano Composition - Glass

Properties of Nano materials:
(a) Mechanical properties

- Very strong and withstand extreme strain.
- Most of the materials fracture on bending because of the presence of more defects, but nanomaterials possess only few defects in the structure.

(b) Electrical properties

- The electrical properties of nanomaterials vary between metallic to semiconducting materials.
- It depends on the diameter of the nanomaterials.
- The very high electrical conductivity of nanomaterial is due to minimum defects in the structure.

(c) Thermal conductivity

- The thermal conductivity of nanomaterials are very high, is due to the vibration of covalent bonds.
- Its thermal conductivity is 10 times greater than the metal.
- The very high thermal conductivity of nanomaterial is also due to minimum defects in the structure.

- Because of these unique and unusual properties, nanomaterials are finding in:
- **Medicine:** diagnostics, drug delivery, synthetic bones.
- **Energy:** energy production, energy saving, fuel cells.
- **Information and Communication Technology:** optoelectronic devices, TV, displays, memory storages.

- **Heavy industry:** construction (nanoparticle in glass, coatings etc.), automotive, aerospace, catalysis.

Summary - Properties of materials
Properties are the way the material responds to the environment and external forces.

- **Mechanical properties** – response to mechanical forces, strength, etc.
- **Electrical and magnetic properties** - response electrical and magnetic fields, conductivity, etc.
- **Thermal properties** are related to transmission of heat and heat capacity.
- **Optical properties** include to absorption, trans-mission and scattering of light.
- **Chemical stability** in contact with the environment - corrosion resistance.

Future of materials

Design of materials having specific desired characteristics directly from our knowledge of atomic structure.

- Miniaturization: "Nanostructured" materials, with microstructure that has length scales between 1 and 100 nanometers with unusual properties. Electronic components, materials for quantum computing.
- Smart materials: airplane wings that adjust to the air flow conditions, buildings that stabilize themselves in earthquakes.
- Environment - friendly materials: biodegradable or photodegradable plastics, advances in nuclear waste processing, etc.
- Learning from Nature: shells and biological hard tissue can be as strong as the most advanced laboratory-produced ceramics, biocompatible adhesives that we do not know how to reproduce...

Testing and Material Testing

- Testing is nothing but, to ensure the specification and ratings of the particular element, component, device and equipment.
- Materials testing is a well-established technique used to determine the physical and mechanical properties of raw materials and components from a human hair to steel, composite materials and ceramics.
- Reproducible evaluation of material properties

1.2 Classification of Material Testing

- Destructive testing or Mechanical testing or Static testing (Chapter II)
- Non Destructive testing or Dynamic testing (Chapter III)
- Material Characterization testing (Chapter IV)
- Thermal Testing (Chapter V)
- Chemical Testing (Chapter V)

1.3 Purpose of Testing

It can support at any stage of production, From assisting in the research and development phase of product development/innovation, Resolving quality issues in the manufacturing process to failure analysis, Expert witness services and regulatory compliance.

Ensure quality

Find the properties

Prevent failure in use

Choices in using materials

Factor of Safety is the ratio comparing the actual stress on a material and the safe useable stress. Tastings are carried out in accordance with national, international and industry standards and regulations, or client specifications

1.4 Selection of material

To choose the optimum combination of properties in a material at the lowest possible cost without compromising the quality.

Factors affecting the selection of materials:

Material Properties

The expected level of performance from the material

Material Cost and Availability

?Material must be priced appropriately (not cheap but right)

?Material must be available (better to have multiple sources)

Processing

?Must consider how to make the part, for example: Casting , Machining, Welding

Environment

?The effect that the service environment has on the part

?The effect the part has on the environment

?The effect that processing has on the environment

1.Availability : The material should be readily available in market in large enough quantities to meet the requirements.

2. Mechanical Properties:

The important mechanical properties of material from the consideration design are strength, rigidity, toughness, resilience,shock resistance, wear resistance, creep characteristics, corrosion resistance, frictional properties and hardness.

3. **Cost**

Cost of Material : The cost of raw material accounts about 50 % of the finished cost

Cost of Processing: The processing cost (labour cost) and other costs such as overhead costs account for about 50% of the production cost

4. Manufacture consideration

It is important consideration in selection of materials. Sometimes, expensive materials are more economical than low cost material, which difficult to machine.

5. Structure - Crystal structure

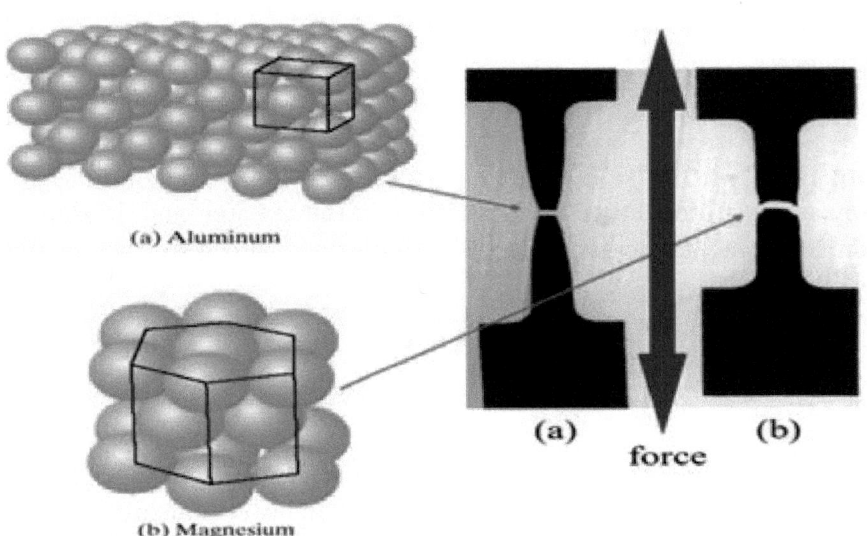

Fig. 7 Crystal Structure

Structure - Microstructure

Different materials exhibit different microstructures and resultant properties
Extrinsic grain boundary dislocations in Al
Sliding of defect free Σ11 {131} grain boundary
Superplastic deformation involves low-stress sliding along grain boundaries, a complex process of which material scientists have limited knowledge and that is a subject of current investigations.

Fig. 8 Microstructure

Material Selection

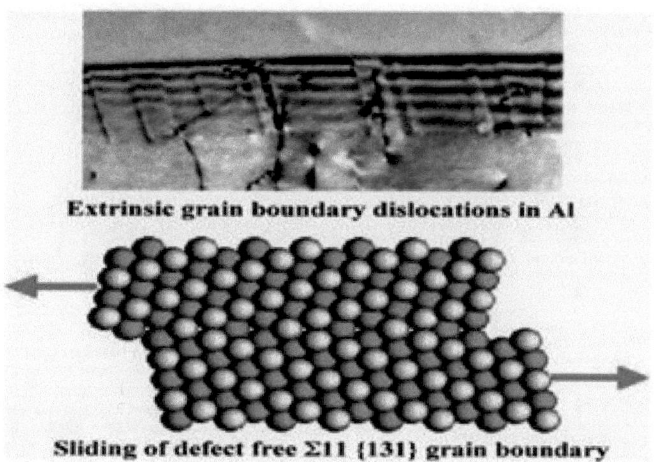

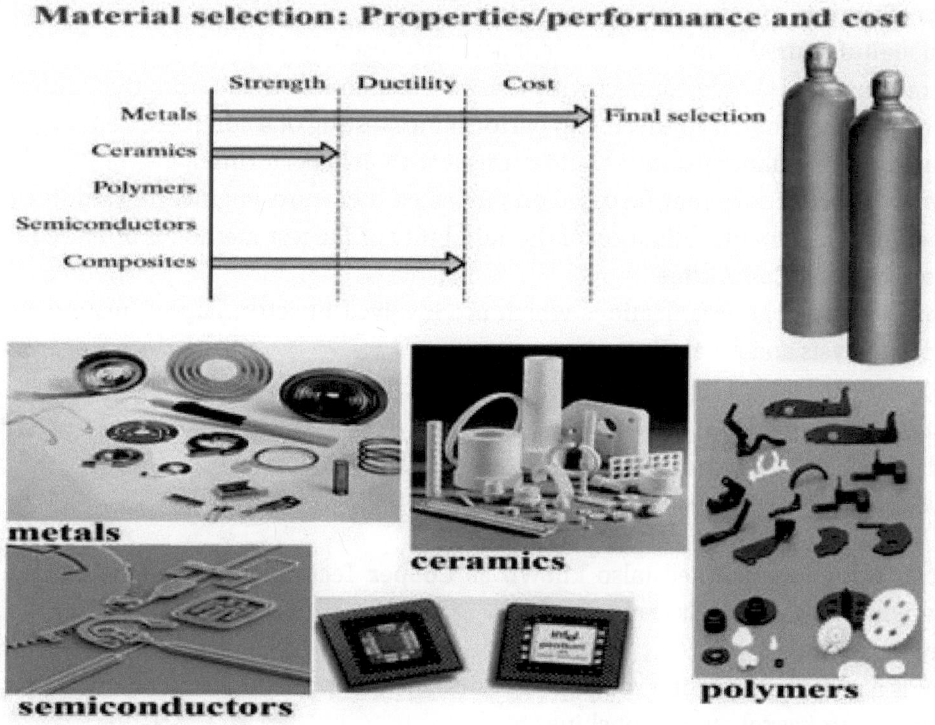
Material selection: Properties/performance and cost
Strength
Ductility
Cost
Metals
Final selection
Ceramics
Polymers
Semiconductors
Composites
metals
ceramics
semiconductors
polymers

Fig. 9 Selection of Materials

Procedure for materials selection:

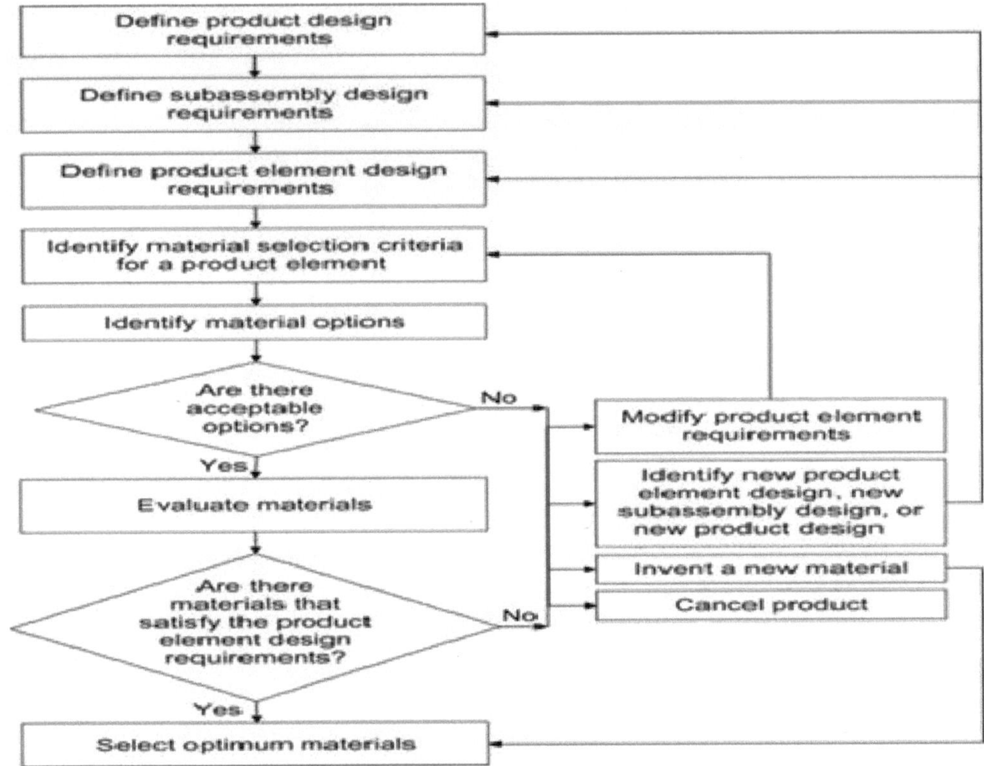

Fig. 10 Flowchart for Material Selection

1.5 Development of testing

For example, if a manufactured item has several components, test methods may have several levels of connections:

test results of a raw material should connect with tests of a component made from that material

test results of a component should connect with performance testing of a complete item

results of laboratory performance testing should connect with field performance

These connections or correlations may be based on published literature, engineering studies, or formal programs such as quality function deployment. Validation of the suitability of the test method is often required.

1.6 Testing Organization & Committee

The following are some global organizations which are involved in setting up of "testing standards" and active research for material analysis and reliability testing.

American Association of Textile Chemists andColorists(AATCC)

American National Standards Institute(ANSI)

American Society of Heating, Refrigerating and AirConditioning Engineers(ASHRAE)

ASTM International (American Society for Testing and Materials)

Cooper Research Technology:

Cooper Research Technology Limited (also known as **Cooper** Technology) is a British manufacturer of high-performance civil engineering materials testing

European Reference Materials

Instron : Instron is a manufacturer of test equipment designed to evaluate the mechanical properties of materials and components, such as universal testing machines.

International Committee for Non Destructive Testing

International Organization for Standardization (ISO)

ISTFA: Useful resources on Material, Device and Failure Analysis

National Physical Laboratory (United Kingdom)

Nadcap (National Aerospace and Defense Contractors Accreditation Program)

MTS Systems Corporation : MTS Systems Corporation is a global supplier of test systems and industrial position sensors. The company provides test and measurement solutions to determine the performance and reliability of vehicles, aircraft, civil structures, biomedical materials and devices and raw materials.

XYZTEC :**XYZTEC** sets the standard in Statistical Process Control (SPC) with 100% focus on science of bond testing .

Zwick Roell Group: The Zwick Roell Group is a manufacturer of static testing machines and systems for materials and components testing.

Following are some international laboratories working in the area of material testing.

Evants Analytical Group

FEI Company

ISTI

Lucideon

Materials Analysis and Technology

Metallurgical Services in Mumbai, India

MicomLaboratories

Razi Metallurgical Research Center, RMRC

Rocky Mountain Laboratories

SEMATECH

Toxicology testing

International Standards are developed by ISO technical committees (TC) and subcommittees (SC) by a process with six steps:

Stage 1: Proposal stage

Stage 2: Preparatory stage

Stage 3: Committee stage

Stage 4: Enquiry stage

Stage 5: Approval stage

Stage 6: Publication stage

Stages in the development process of an ISO standard

Stage	Associated document name	Abbreviations
Preliminary	Preliminary work item	PWI
Proposal	New work item proposal	• NP or NWIP • NP Amd/TR/TS/IWA
Preparatory	Working draft or drafts	• AWI • AWI Amd/TR/TS • WD • WD Amd/TR/TS
Committee	Committee draft or drafts	• CD • CD Amd/Cor/TR/TS • PDAmd (PDAM) • PDTR • PDTS
Approval	Final draft	FDIS FDAmd
Publication	International Standard	ISO TR TS
Review		IWA Amd Cor

Table 1. ISO Procedure standard

1.7 Testing Standards

This is a list of ASTM International standards.

Standard designations usually consist of a letter prefix and a sequentially assigned number.

This may optionally be followed by a dash and the last two digits of the year in which the standard was adopted. eg. C1634-90

Prefix letters correspond to the following subjects:

A = Iron and Steel Materials

B = Nonferrous Metal Materials

C = Ceramic, Concrete, and Masonry Materials

D = Miscellaneous Materials

E = Miscellaneous Subjects

F = Materials for Specific Applications ·

G = Corrosion, Deterioration, and Degradation of Materials

This list may include either current or withdrawn standards. A withdrawn standard has been discontinued by its sponsoring committee. A standard may be withdrawn with or without replacement.

1.8 Result Analysis of Testing

Testing is vital part of any engineering design and manufacturing process in related to product and its application. Key benefits of Result analyses includes characterization of material properties, validation/confirmation of product function, validation of computer simulations, provision of empirical data to refine and improve simulations, proof of iterative product improvement, clear, visible evidence of product integrity to clients.

Testing is investment –A significant amount of product testing requires specialist or bespoke equipment and skilled engineers to design the test, its equipment and to accurately analyses the result. However using dedicated **test** house can provide **cost effective** option for companies looking for professionally executed, reliable and accurate test program. Testing analysis is used to optimize the product and develop new technologies.

1.9 Advantages of Testing

Reduction of repetitive work: Repetitive work is very boring if it is done manually,

Examples of this type of repetitive work include running regression tests, entering the same test data again and again

Greater consistency and repeatability: People have tendency to do the same task in a slightly different way even when they think they are repeating something exactly. A tool will exactly reproduce what it did before, so each time it is run the result is consistent.

Objective assessment: If a person calculates a value from the software or incident reports, by mistake they may omit something, or their own one-sided preconceived judgments or convictions may lead them to interpret that data incorrectly.

Examples include assessing the cyclamate complexity or nesting levels of a component (which can be done by a static analysis tool), coverage (coverage measurement tool), system behavior (monitoring tools) and incident statistics (test management tool).

Ease of access to information about tests or testing: Information presented visually is much easier for the human mind to understand and interpret.

For example, a chart or graph is a better way to show information than a long list of numbers – this is why charts and graphs in spreadsheets are so useful. Special purpose tools give these features directly for the information they process. Examples include statistics and graphs about test progress (test execution or test management tool), incident rates (incident management or test management tool) and performance (performance testing tool).

1.10 Importance of Testing

Testing is performed for a variety of reasons and can provide a wealth of information about the tested materials, prototypes or product samples. some of the reasons why material testing is important:

Meeting requirements of regulatory agencies

Selecting appropriate materials and treatments for an application

Evaluating product design or improvement specifications

Verifying a production process

Regulatory compliance

Many products are used in critical applications where a failure could result in extensive damage or injury. Some examples are manufactured fasteners and parts that have a vital role in maintaining the safety of aircraft, bridges, vehicles, nuclear reactors, military equipment and medical implants. In addition, many jurisdictions have adopted legislation restricting the use of hazardous materials. In cases like these, governments and regulatory bodies set compliance requirements that must be met by manufacturers. Companies must adhere to these standards, which generally specify test procedures, to prove compliance.

Material and treatment selection

The quality of a material going into a manufactured product is as important as the reliability of the production process. With the wide variety of materials and treatments available in the marketplace, testing can help narrow down the choices to the most appropriate selection for the intended use. As mentioned before, for many industry applications, testing is performed to certify material to a given standard or specification, or to verify that it meets other stringent criteria before it is put into use. It may also make sense to verify the composition or elemental content of the material with an instrumental or classical wet chemicalanalysistechnique.

Product design and improvement

It'stypicalforabusinesstopurchasemechanical testingserviceswhenspecifyingmaterialforanew product design. When an application requires more durable or more corrosion-resistant metals, this can often be attained with the addition of treatments. When appropriate, the material may be heat treated prior to testing to determine that the specified results have been achieved. In further determining material characteristics, microanalysis, using microscopes and SEM equipment, can be used to analyze various surface features and to detect flaws and inconsistencies.

Production processes

Testing is an essential part of both design and manufacturing processes, not only when safety is a concern, but also for any company committed to selling reliable products and minimizing damage and costs if problems do surface. Testing is often performed early on during product development to evaluate a planned production process. It can also be just as relevant to provide validation for final products on an ongoing basis. Materialstestingalsoplaysalargeroleinfailure analysisinvestigationstohelpidentifydefectiveproducts, inadequate materials and, ultimately, the cause of a failure. When materials testing services are purchased from an independent laboratory like Laboratory Testing Inc., a certified test report is provided that documents applicable accreditations, specifications/standards, other test criteria and complete test results.

TWO
MECHANICAL TESTING

2.1. INTRODUCTION TO MECHANICAL TESTING

Mechanical properties are obtained by mechanical testing. Mechanical testing is used for developing design data, maintaining quality control, assisting in alloy development programs and providing data in failure analysis.

Mechanical testing is usually destructive and requires test specimens of the material to be machined or cut to the specific shape required by the test method.

2.1.1 TYPES OF MECHANICAL TESTING

There exists a large number of tests, many of which are standardized, to determine the various mechanical properties of materials. In general, such tests set out to obtain geometry-independent properties; i.e. those intrinsic to the bulk material. In practice this is not always feasible, since even in tensile tests, certain properties can be influenced by specimen size and/or geometry. Here is a listing of some of the most common tests

- Hardness Testing
    - Brinell hardness test (HB)
    - Rockwell hardness test (HR), principally used in the USA
    - Vickers hardness test (HV), which has one of the widest scales
    - Knoop hardness test (HK), for measurement over small areas
    - Janka hardness test, for wood
    - Meyer hardness test
    - Shore durometer hardness, used for polymers
    - Barcol hardness test, for composite materials
- Tensile testing, used to obtain the stress-strain curve for a material, and from there, properties such as Young modulus, yield (or proof) stress, tensile stress and % elongation to failure.
- Impact testing
    - Izod test
    - Charpy test
- Fracture toughness testing
    - Linear-elastic (KIc)*
    - K–R curve
    - Elastic plastic (JIc, CTOD)
- Creep Testing, for the mechanical behaviour of materials at high temperatures (relative to their melting point)

- Fatigue Testing, for the behaviour of materials under cyclic loading

  - Load-controlled smooth specimen tests
  - Strain-controlled smooth specimen tests

Fatigue crack growth testing

2.1.2 Types of mechanical properties

Mechanical Properties

- Describe material when a force is applied to it.
- Determined through testing, usually involving destruction of material.
- Extremely important to consider in design.

a)Ductility
b)Toughness
c)Brittleness
d)Hardness
e)Plasticity
f)Elasticity
g)Strength

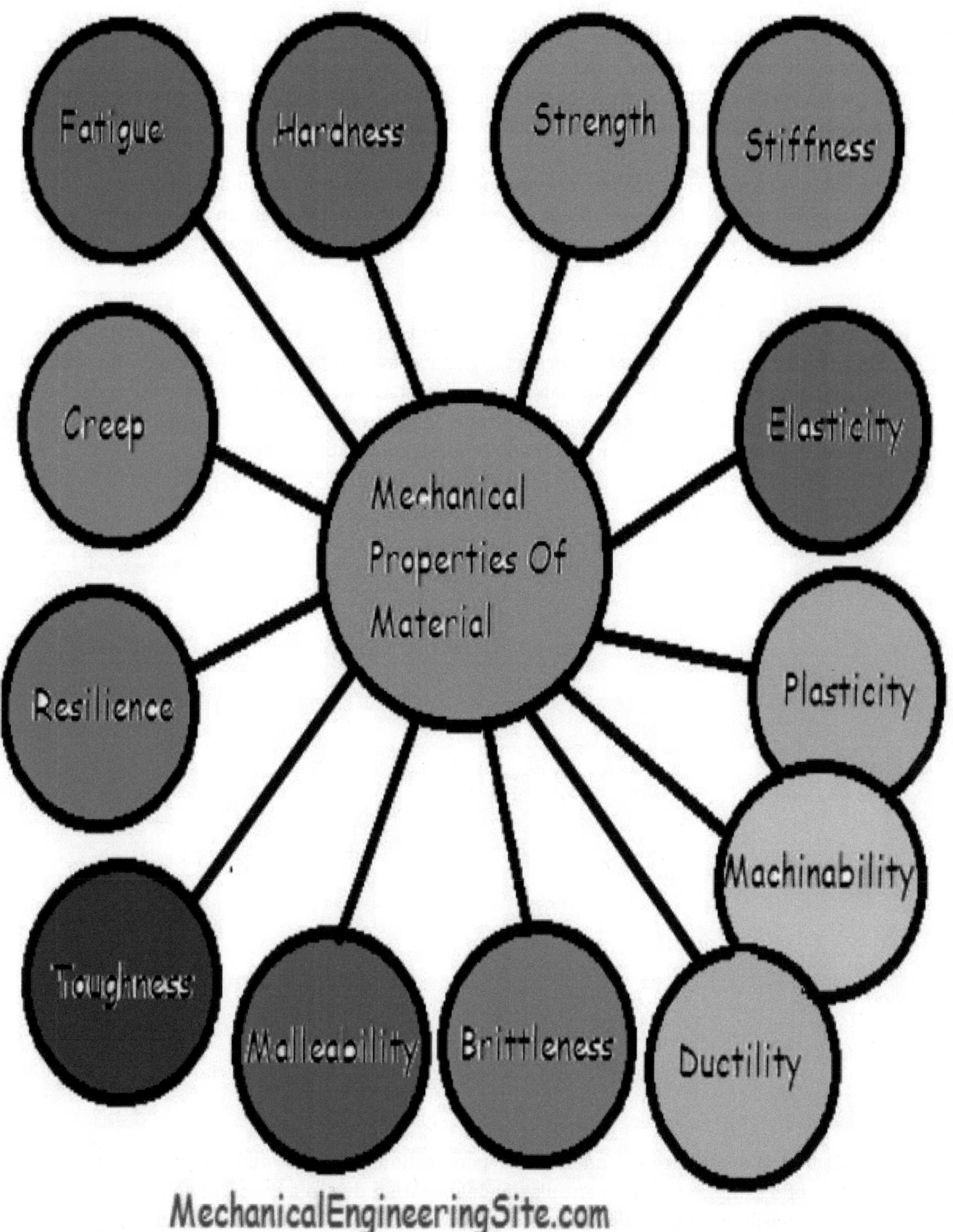

Fig. 2.1 Mechanical Testing Property

Ductility

It is a solid material's ability to deform under tensile stress; this is often characterized by the material's ability to be stretched into a wire.

Ductility is termed as the property of amaterial enabling it to be drawn into wire with theapplication of tensile load. The ductility is usually measured by the terms,

Percentage elongation and percent reduction inarea which is often used as empirical measures of ductility. The materials those possess more than 5%elongation are called as ductile materials.

Toughness

Toughness is the ability of a material to absorb energy and plastically deform without fracturing

Material toughness is defined as the amount of energy per volume that a material can absorb before rupturing. It is also defined as the resistance to fracture of a material when stressed. Toughness requires a balance of strength and ductility.

Brittleness

A material is **brittle** if, when subjected to stress, it breaks without significant deformation (strain).

Brittle materials absorb relatively little energy prior to fracture, even those of high strength. Breaking is often accompanied by a snapping sound. Brittle materials include most ceramics and glasses (which do not deform plastically) and some polymers, such as PMMA and polystyrene. Many steels become brittle at low temperatures (see ductile-brittle transition temperature), depending on their composition and processing.

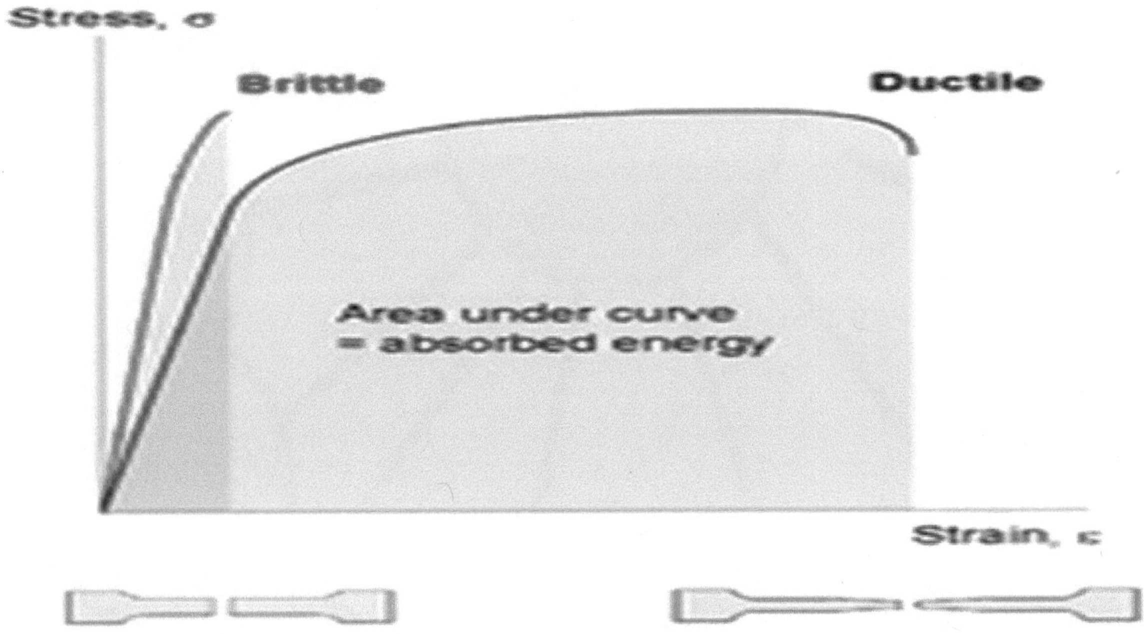

Fig. 2.2 Stress and Strain Curve for Brittle and Ductile Material

Hardness

Hardness is the degree of resistance to indentation, penetration, abrasion and wear. Indentation hardness measures the resistance of a sample to permanent plastic deformation due to a constant compression load from a sharp object; they are primarily used in engineering and metallurgy fields. The tests work on the basic premise of measuring the critical dimensions of an indentation left by a specifically dimensioned and loaded indenter. Common indentation hardness scales are Rockwell, Vickers, Shore, and Brinell.

Plasticity

Plasticity is defined the mechanicalproperty of a material which retains thedeformation produced under load permanently. This property of the material is required in forging, instamping images on coins. It is the ability ortendency of material to undergo some degree ofpermanent deformation without its rupture or its failure. Plasticity is the propensity of a material to undergo permanent deformation under load.

Elasticity

It is defined as the property of a materialto regain its original shape after deformation whenthe external forces are removed.It can also be referred as the power of material tocome back to its original position after deformationwhen the stress or load is removed. It is also calledas the tensile property of the material. Elasticity(or **stretchiness**) is the physical property of a material that returns to its original shape after the stress (e.g. external forces) that made it deform or distort is removed. The relative amount of deformation is called the strain.

Strength

Strength is the ability of a material to withstand various loads to which it is subjected during a test or service. Strength is defined as the ability ofmaterial to resist the externally applied forces orstresses without fracture.This property of material therefore determines the

Ability to withstand stress without failure. The maximum stress that any material canwithstand before destruction is called its ultimatestrength. The tenacity of the material is its ultimatestrength in tension.

Fatigue – The failure of a material caused underrepeated loads or stresses is known as fatigue orfatigue failure.

Toughness- toughness is the amount of energy thata material can absorb before it fractures.It is desirable property for structural and machineparts which have to withstand shock and vibration.

Resilience – resilience is the capacity of a materialto absorb or store energy, and to resist shock andimpact.

Weldability-Weldability is defined as the property ofa metal which indicates the two similar or dissimilarmetals are joined by fusion with or without theapplication of pressure and with or without the useof filler metal (welding) efficiently.

Castability-Castability is defined as the property ofmetal, which indicates the ease with it can becasted into different shapes and sizes. Cast iron,aluminum and brass are possessing goodcastability.

Workability or Formability- It is the property ofmetals which denotes the ease in its forming in tovarious shapes and sizes. The different factors that affect the formability arecrystal structure of metal, grain size of metal hotand cold working, alloying element present in theparent metal. Hot working increases formability. Low carbon steelpossesses good formability.

Creep- When a metal part when is subjected to ahigh constant stress at high temperature for a longerperiod of time, it will undergo a slow and permanentdeformation (in form of a crack which may furtherpropagate further towards creep failure) calledcreep.

Malleability - Malleability is the ability of thematerial to be flattened into thin sheets underapplications of heavy compressive forces withoutcracking by hot or cold working means. It is a special case of ductility which permitsmaterials to be rolled or hammered into thin sheets.

Yield point- At a specific stress, ductile metalsparticularly ceases, offering resistance to tensileforces.

Stiffness- It is defined as the ability of a material toresist deformation under stress. The resistance of amaterial to elastic deformation or deflection iscalled stiffness or rigidity.

2.2. HARDNESS TEST

Hardness has a variety of meanings. To the metals industry, it may bethought of as resistance to permanent deformation. To the metallurgist, itmeans resistance to penetration. To the lubrication engineer, it means resistanceto wear. To the design engineer, it is a measure of flow stress. To themineralogist, it means resistance to scratching, and to the machinist, itmeans resistance to machining. Hardness may also be referred to as meancontact pressure. All of these characteristics are related to the plastic flowstress of materials.

Indentation hardness measures the resistance of a sample to permanent plastic deformation due to a constant compression load from a sharp object. Hardness is defined as the ability of a metal to cut another metal. A harder metal canalways cut or put impression to the softer metals byvirtue of its hardness. It embraces many different properties such asresistance to wear, scratching, deformation andmachinability etc. The hardness test is a mechanical test for material properties which are used 2.in engineering design, analysis of structures, and materials development. The principal purpose of the hardness test is to determine the suitability of a material for a given application, or the particular treatment to which the material has been subjected. The ease with which the hardness test can be made has made it the most common method of inspection for metals and alloys.

Hardness is defined as the resistance of a material to permanent deformation such as indentation, wear, abrassion, scratch. Principally, the importance of hardness testing has to do with the relationship between hardness and other properties of material. For example, both the hardness test and the tensile test measure the resistance of a metal to plastic flow, and results of these tests may closely parallel each other. The hardness test is preferred because it is simple, easy, and relatively nondestructive.

2.2.1 Types of Harness Test

Hardness is indicated in a variety of ways, as indicated by the names of thetests that follow:

- *Static indentation tests:* A ball, cone, or pyramid is forced into the surfaceof the metal being tested. The relationship of load to the area ordepth of indentation is the measure of hardness, such as in Brinell,Knoop, Rockwell, and Vickers hardness tests.
- *Rebound tests:* An object of standard mass and dimensions is bouncedfrom the surface of the workpiece being tested, and the height of reboundis the measure of hardness. The Scleroscope and Leeb tests are examples.
- *Scratch file tests:* The idea is that one material is capable of scratchinganother. The Mohs and file hardness tests are examples of this type.
- *Plowing tests:* A blunt element (usually diamond) is moved across thesurface of the workpiece being tested under controlled conditions of load and shape. The width of the groove is the measure of hardness. TheBierbaum test is an example.
- *Damping tests:* Hardness is determined by the change in amplitude of apendulum having a hard pivot, which rests on the surface of theworkpiece being tested. The Herbert Pendulum test is an example.
- *Cutting tests:* A sharp tool of given shape is caused to remove a chip ofstandard dimensions from the surface of the workpiece being tested.
- *Abrasion tests:* A workpiece is loaded against a rotating disk, and therate of wear is the measure of hardness.
- *Erosion tests:* Sand or other granular abrasive is impinged on the surfaceof the workpiece being tested under standard conditions, and loss of materialin a given time is the measure of hardness. Hardness of grindingwheels is measured by this testing method.
- *Electromagnetic testing:* Hardness is measured as a variable againststandards of known flux density.
- *Ultrasonic testing:* A type of indentation test

However,the focus is on static indentation tests, because they are the most widelyused. Rebound testing is also used extensively, particularly for hardnessmeasurements on large workpieces or for applications in which visible orsharp impressions in the test surface cannot be tolerated. Current practice divides hardness testing into two categories: macrohardness and microhardness. Macrohardness refers to testing with applied loads on the indenter of more than 1 kg and covers, for example, the testing of tools, dies, and sheet material in the heavier gages. In microhardness testing, applied loads are 1 kg and below, and material being tested is very thin (down to 0.0125 mm, or 0.0005 in.). Applications include extremely small parts, thin superficially hardened parts, plated surfaces, and individual constituents of materials.

1) Macro Hardness Testers Loads > 1 kg

(a) Rockwell

(b) Brinell

(c) Vickers

2) Micro Hardness Testers < 1 kg

Knoop diamond

Vickers diamond pyramid

(a) Rockwell Hardness Test

The Rockwell Hardness Test is generally a non-destructive test performed on samples when it is necessary to determine how hard a material is. Hugh M. Rockwell (1890–1957) and Stanley P. Rockwell (1886–1940) from Connecticut co-invented the first tester and a patent was granted in 1919. The Rockwell Hardness test is generally considered easier to perform compared to other methods such as Vickers or Brinell. Stanley P. Rockwell invented the Rockwell hardness test. He was a metallurgist for a large ball bearing company and he wanted a fast non-destructive way to determine if the heat treatment process they were doing on the bearing races was successful. The Vickers test was too time consuming, Brinell indents were too big for his parts and the Scleroscope was difficult to use, especially on his small parts. To satisfy his needs he invented the Rockwell test method.

Hardness is defined as a material's resistance to permanent indentation. Current Rockwell Hardness test methods are specified in ASTM E-18 and anyone wishing to perform a Rockwell Hardness test should become familiar with this test standard

1 Purpose of Rockwell test

Rockwell is a fast method, developed tobe used for production control and has a direct readout. This simple sequence of test force application proved to be a major advance in the world of hardness testing. It enabled the user to perform an accurate hardness test on a variety of sized parts in just a few seconds. The Rockwell hardness (HR) is calculated by measuring thedepth of an indent, after an indenter hasbeen forced into the specimen material at a given load. The indenter material is aconical diamond, or sintered carbide ball, depending on the scale being used. A minor preload is applied before the mainload is put on and there after unloaded.

The readout of the hardness value is performedwhile the minor pre-load is still applied, Generally, the tested material shouldnot be mounted in resin, because theRockwell test uses the motion of the indenter to measure the hardness and not the indentation area. The influence hereofhowever depends on the machine used.

2. Principle and Procedure of the Rockwell Test

1. The indenter moves down into position on the part surface
2. A minor load is applied and a zero reference position is established
3. The major load is applied for a specified time period (dwell time) beyond zero
4. The major load is released leaving the minor load applied

The resulting Rockwell number represents the difference in depth from the zero reference position as a result of the application of the major load.

The Rockwell hardness test method consists of indenting the test material with a diamond cone or hardened steel ball indenter. The indenter is forced into the test material under a preliminary minor load ?0 usually 10 kgf. When equilibrium has been reached, an indicating device, which follows the movements of the indenter and so responds to changes in depth of penetration of the indenter is set to a datum

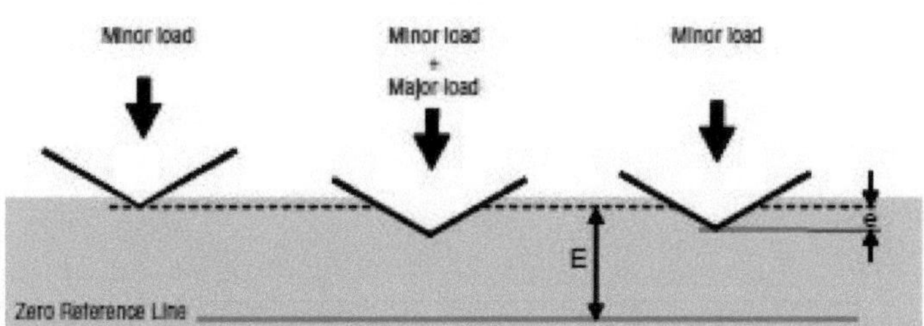

Fig. 2.3 Hardness Test

position. While the preliminary minor load is still applied an additional major load is applied with resulting increase in penetration. When equilibrium has again been reach, the additional major load is removed but the preliminary minor load is still maintained. Removal of the additional major load allows a partial recovery, so reducing the depth of penetration. The permanent increase in depth of penetration, resulting from the application and removal of the additional major load is used to calculate the Rockwell hardness number.

3. Rockwell Hardness Test Procedure

The Rockwell hardness test consists of indenting the test material with a diamond cone or hardened steel ball indenter. Each time a test is performed two loads are applied to the sample being tested. First, the indenter is forced into the test material under a preliminary minor load and this depth is recorded. With the minor load still applied an additional load is introduced known as the major load which increases the depth of penetration on the sample. The Major load is then removed, and the force on the sample is returned to the minor load. The increase in the depth of penetration that results from applying and removing the major load is used to calculate the Rockwell hardness value.

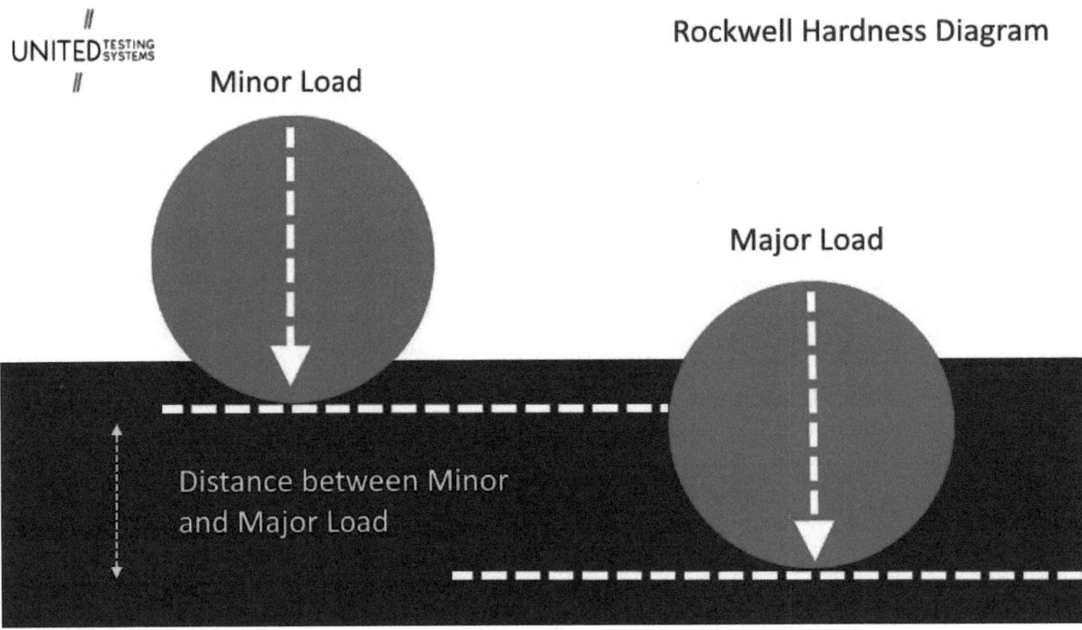

Fig. 2.4 Rockwell Hardness Test

2.5. Rockwell Hardness Scales

Rockwell hardness values are expressed as a combination of a hardness number and a scale symbol representing the indenter and the minor and major loads. The hardness number is expressed by the symbol HR and the scale designation. There are several different Rockwell Scales each denoted by a single letter. Each scale requires different loads or indenters, so careful consideration should be given to which scale you are working with when evaluating results.

Scale	Abbreviation
A	HRA
B	HRB
C	HRC
D	HRD
E	HRE
F	HRF
G	HRG
H	HRH

Table 2.1 Rockwell Testing Scale

There are 30 different scales. The majority of applications are covered by the Rockwell C and B scales for testing steel, brass, and other metals. However, the increasing use of materials other than steel and brass as well as thin materials necessitates a basic knowledge of the factors that must be considered in choosing the correct scale to ensure an accurate Rockwell test. The choice is not only between the regular hardness test and superficial hardness test, with three different major loads for each, but also between the diamond indenter and the 1/16, 1/8, 1/4 and 1/2 in. diameter steel ball indenters.

For soft materials such as copper alloys, soft steel, and aluminum alloys a 1/16" diameter steel ball is used with a 100-kilogram load and the hardness is read on the "B" scale. In testing harder materials, hard cast iron and many steel alloys, a 120 degrees diamond cone is used with up to a 150 kilogram load and the hardness is read on the "C" scale. There are several Rockwell scales other than the "B" & "C" scales, (which are called the common scales). A properly reported Rockwell value will have the hardness number followed by "HR" (Hardness Rockwell) and the scale letter. For example, 50 HRB indicates that the material has a hardness reading of 50 on the B scale.

If no specification exists or there is doubt about the suitability of the specified scale, an analysis should be made of the following factors that control scale selection:

- Type of material
- Specimen thickness
- Test location
- Scale limitations

Superficial Scales

The Rockwell Hardness test also uses superficial scales. These use lower loads and shallower indentions when a sample may be too brittle or thin for a standard Rockwell Hardness Test.

Superficial Rockwell hardness tester: 15N, 30N, 45N, 15T, 30T, 45T, 15W, 30W, 45W, 15X, 30X, 45X, 15Y, 30Y, 45Y

Polymer/Plastic Scales

There are also Rockwell Hardness Scales used for polymers and plastics. Those are scales R, L, M, E and K. Like other scales different sized indenters are used depending on the scale.

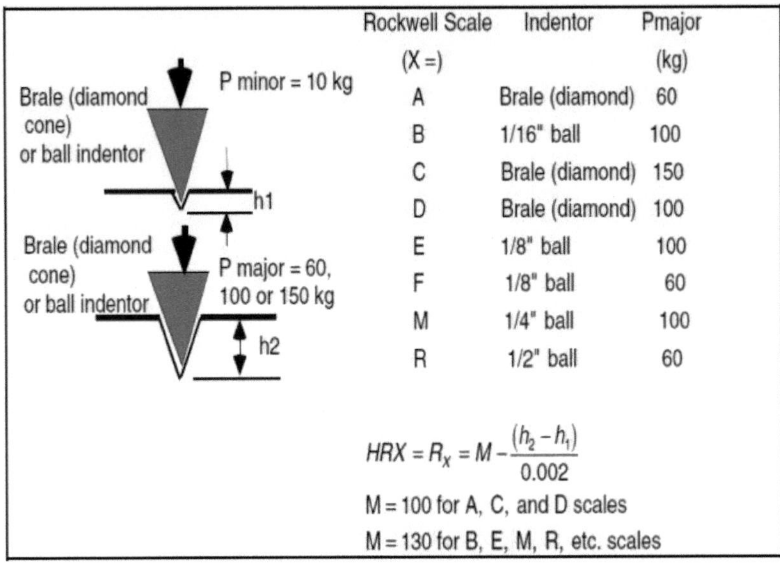

Fig. 2.5 Hardness Test Superficial Scales

Constraints for Rockwell hardness test

- Require clean and well positioned indenter and anvil
- The test sample should be clean, dry, smooth and oxide-free surface
- Low reading of hardness value might be expected in cylindrical surfaces
- Specimen thickness should be 10 times higher than the depth of the indenter
- The spacing between the indentations should be 3 to 5 times of the indentation diameter
- Loading speed should be standardized.

Applications

Rockwell can be used for most materials but typically only for larger sized specimens due to the high loads and the indenters used.

(b) The Brinell Hardness Test

Dr. J. A. Brinell invented the Brinell test in Sweden in 1900. The oldest of the hardness test methods in common use today, the Brinell test is frequently used to determine the hardness of forgings and castings that have a grain structure too course for Rockwell or Vickers testing. Therefore, Brinell tests are frequently done on large parts. By varying the test force and ball size, nearly all metals can be tested using a Brinell test. Brinell values are considered test force independent as long as the ball size/test force relationship is the same. In the USA, Brinell testing is typically done on iron and steel castings using a 3000 Kg test force and a 10 mm diameter carbide ball. Aluminum and other softer alloys are frequently tested using a 500 Kg test force and a 10 or 5mm carbide ball. Therefore the typical range of Brinell testing in this country is 500 to 3000kg with 5 or 10mm carbide balls. In Europe Brinell testing is done using a much wider range of forces and ball sizes. It's common in Europe to perform Brinell tests on small parts using a 1 mm carbide ball and a test force as low as 1kg. These low load tests are commonly referred to as baby Brinell tests. Brinell (HBW)

Brinell indentation gives a relatively large impression with a tungsten carbide ball, denotation HBW (W is the chemical symbol for tungsten). The size of the indent is read optically in order to determine the hardness. Typical applications are forgings and castings where the structural elements are large and inhomogeneous or structures too coarse for other methods (Rockwell/ Vickers) to give a representative result.

Load Range: 1-3000 kgf

Indenter Types: 1 / 2.5 / 5 / 10 mm diameter balls.

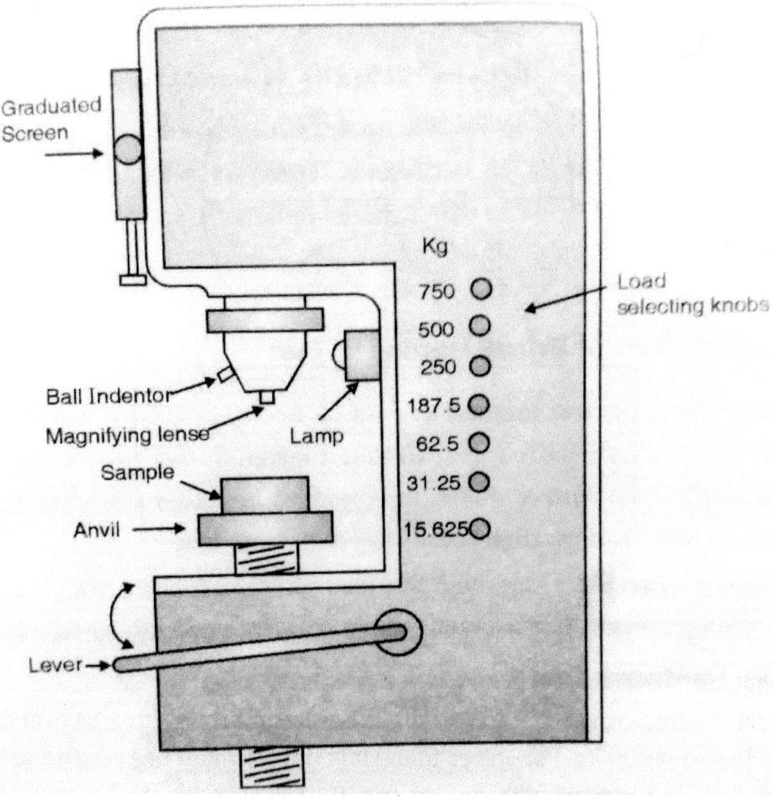

Fig. 2.6. Brinell indentation

1. PRINCIPLE OF BRINELL TEST

Brinell Hardness Test is one of the most important hardness tests in the engineering industry and metallurgy. It is used when the surface of the metal is very rough to use another hardness test on it. There are two methods to perform the Brinell hardness Test on the metal as follows:

1. Standard Method
2. Non-Standard Method

Standard BrinellHardness Test:

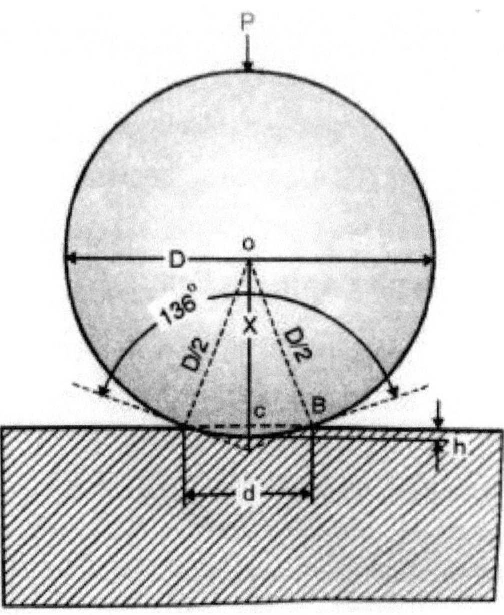

Fig. 2.7 Brinell Indentation

Brinell Indentation Diagram

The Brinell hardness test method consists of indenting the test material with a 10 mm diameter hardened steel or carbide ball subjected to a load of 3000 kg. For softer materials the load can be reduced to 1500 kg or 500 kg to avoid excessive indentation. The full load is normally applied for 10 to 15 seconds in the case of iron and steel and for at least 30 seconds in the case of other metals. The diameter of the indentation left in the test material is measured with a low powered microscope. The Brinell harness number is calculated by dividing the load applied by the surface area of the indentation. When the indentor is retracted two diameters of the impression, d_1 and d_2 , are measured using a microscope with a calibrated graticule and then averaged as shown in *Fig.* 2.8

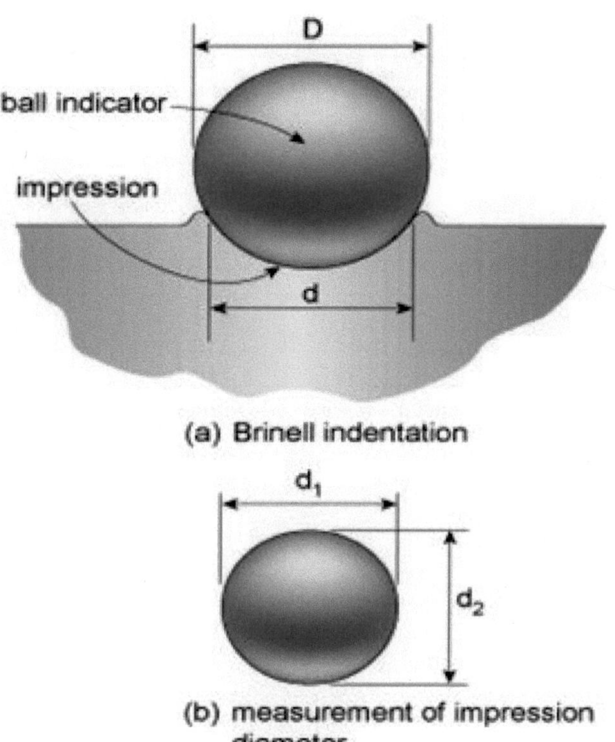

(a) Brinell indentation

(b) measurement of impression diameter

Fig. 2.8.

In the standard method of the Brinell Hardness Test, we use 250 to 500 kg of load for soft material and 500 to 3000 kg of load for hard material such as steel and iron. In the standard method of the test, we use a ball indenter of 10mm diameter. Let's derive the formula of Brinell Hardness Number (BHN) for the Brinell Hardness Test.

B.H.N = Load Applied (Kg)/Area of Indentation

B.H.N= $P/\pi Dh$

but, $h = D\text{-}X/2$ —— eq (1)

From the above figure, ΔOCB, we can say that,

$OB^2 = OC^2 + CB^2$

$(D/2)^2 = X^2 + (d/2)^2$

By solving the above equation for X, we get,

$X = \sqrt{(D^2 - d^2)}/2$

$\therefore\ h = D - \sqrt{(D^2 - d^2)}/2$

From eq (1), put the value of h,

$\therefore \pi Dh = \pi D(D - \sqrt{D^2 - d^2})/2$

the above equation is of **the area of indentation.**

Therefore,

$BHN = 2P/\pi D(D - \sqrt{D^2 - d^2})$ —— eq (2)

Where, P =Load in Kg

D = Diameter of the indenter in square mm.

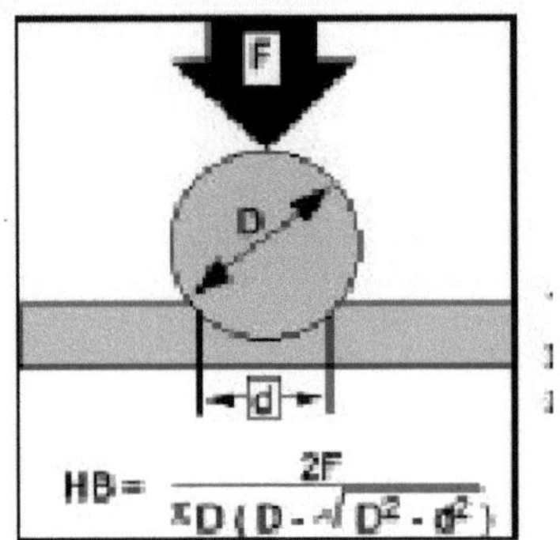

Fig. 2.9 Intention Test

where: HB = the Brinell hardness number F = the imposed load in kg D = the diameter of the spherical indenter in mm d = diameter of the resulting indenter impression in mm. The Brinell number, which normally ranges from HB 50 to HB 750 for metals, will increase as the sample gets harder. Tables are available to make the calculation simple

Non-Standard BrinellHardness Test:

In the non-standard Brinell Hardness Test, we use approximately 100 to 250 kg of load. In this method, we use a ball indenter of 1, 2.5 and 5mm diameter. Due to low load and less ball diameter, this test is used in commercial practices.

Above you can see the diagram of Brinell hardness testing machine equipped with various loads and multiple ball indentors. A load selecting knob is used to change the size of the load. The lever is used to move metal samples in an upward and downward direction. Metal samples are placed over the anvil and a lamp is fixed on the machine column to observe the process.

As we know that, Brinell hardness number (BHN) depends on the load. During the indentation process, the ball indentor does not make a constant angle with the sample surface. This indentor ball makes a large contact angle with the lower load which forms a small impression on the metal sample which resulted in less hardness.

Same as above, the indentor ball makes a small contact angle with a higher load which forms a bigger impression on the metal sample which resulted in more hardness. Therefore it concludes that Brinell hardness number (BHN) is dependent on the load applied.

According to the above observation,

$d = D \sin\theta$

Substitute the above value of d in eq (2), we get,

$BHN = 2P/(\pi)\, D^2\, (1 - \cos\theta)$

We get the equation of BHN for the Non-Standard Brinell Hardness Test.

Advantages of BrinellHardness Test:

- The flat irregular metal surface does not affect the Brinell hardness test.
- This hardness test is less sensitive.
- It is used to measure the hardness of components made from powder metallurgy and cast.
- It can bear the heavy load for testing.
- Indentation made on the sample can be seen and measure under a microscope or eyepiece.
- One scale covers the entire hardness range, although comparable results can only be obtained if the ball size and test force relationship is the same.
- A wide range of test forces and ball sizes to suit every application.
- "Nondestructive", sample can normally be reused.

Disadvantages of BrinellHardness Test:

- The main disadvantage of this test is that it is not suitable for small size objects due to large indentor impression.
- The main drawback of the Brinell test is the need to optically measure the indent size. This requires that the test point be finished well enough to make an accurate measurement.
- Slow. Testing can take 30 seconds not counting the sample preparation time.
- Slightly inaccurate hardness measurement while testing hard objects as ball indentor deforms.
- Not suitable for thin objects due to deep penetration.
- This test can only perform on the flat surfaces.
- The Brinell hardness test is slow thus time-consuming.
- Chances of human error during measurements.
- The Components life may reduce because of high load and large impressions.

Applications of BrinellHardness Test:

- The Brinell hardness test is defined in ASTM E10 is used to calculate Brinell hardness of the metal.
- It is used on the metal having a rough surface and harsh texture.
- The Brinell hardness test is used to measure the hardness of light metals like lead and tin, also hard metals like steel and iron.
- Because of the wide test force range the Brinell test can be used on almost any metallic material. The part size is only limited by the testing instrument's capacity.
- Brinell is suitable for inhomogeneous metals and metals containing coarse structural elements, as for example castings and forgings. Limited to larger specimens due to high loads and indenters used – in particular cast irons, steel and aluminium.

(C) **VICKERS HARDNESS TEST**

The Vickers hardness test was developed in 1921 by Robert L. Smith and George E. Sandland at Vickers Ltd as an alternative to the Brinell method to measure the hardness of materials. The Vickers test is often easier to use than other hardness tests since the required calculations are independent of the size of the indenter, and the indenter can be used for all materials irrespective of hardness.

1 Procedure and principle of vickers hardness

The Vickers hardness test method consists of indenting the test material with a diamond indenter, in the form of a right pyramid with a square base and an angle of 136 degrees between opposite faces subjected to a load of 1 to 100 kgf. The full load is normally applied for 10 to 15 seconds. The two diagonals of the indentation left in the surface of the material after removal of the load are measured using a microscope and their average calculated. The area of the sloping surface of the indentation is calculated. The Vickers hardness is the quotient obtained by dividing the kgf load by the square mm area of indentation.

The basic principle, as with all common measures of hardness, is to observe a material's ability to resist plastic deformation from a standard source. The Vickers test can be used for all metals and has one of the widest scales among hardness tests. The unit of hardness given by the test is known as the Vickers Pyramid Number (HV) or Diamond Pyramid Hardness (DPH). The hardness number can be converted into units of pascals, but should not be confused with pressure, which uses the same units. The hardness number is determined by the load over the surface area of the indentation and not the area normal to the force, and is therefore not pressure.

It was decided that the indenter shape should be capable of producing geometrically similar impressions, irrespective of size; the impression should have well-defined points of measurement; and the indenter should have high resistance to self-deformation. A diamond in the form of a square-based pyramid satisfied these conditions. It had been established that the ideal size of a Brinell impression was $\frac{3}{8}$ of the ball diameter. As two tangents to the circle at the ends of a chord $3d/8$ long intersect at 136°, it was decided to use this as the included angle between plane faces of the indenter tip. This gives an angle from each face normal to the horizontal plane normal of 22° on each side. The angle was varied experimentally and it was found that the hardness value obtained on a homogeneous piece of material remained constant, irrespective of load.The Vickers Hardness (HV) is calculatedby measuring the diagonal lengths ofan indent left by introducing a diamondpyramid indenter with a given load intothe sample material, see Figure. Thesize of the indent is read optically in orderto determine the hardness. The hardnessvalue can be obtained from a tableor formula after determining the meanvalue of the two measured diagonals ordirectly in an automatic hardness tester.

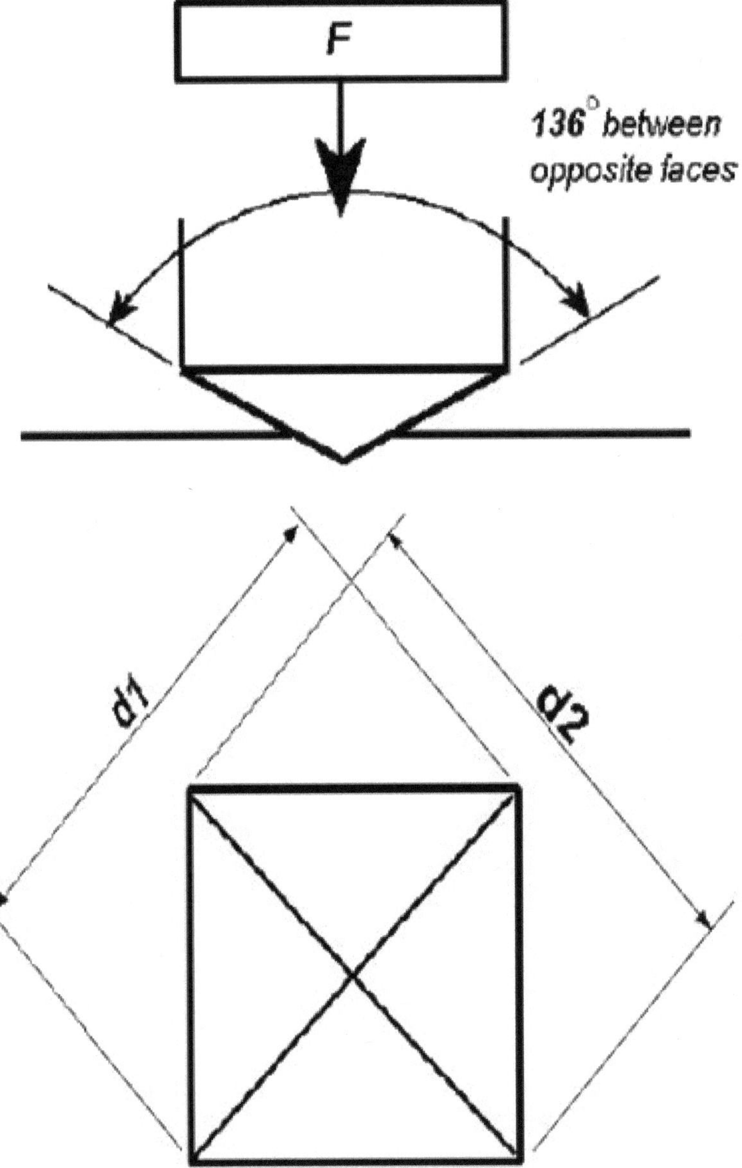

Fig. 2.10. Vickers Test

Accordingly, loads of various magnitudes are applied to a flat surface, depending on the hardness of the material to be measured. The HV number is then determined by the ratio *F/A*, where *F* is the force applied to the diamond in kilograms-force and *A* is the surface area of the resulting indentation in square millimeters. *A* can be determined by the formula

$A = d^2/2 \sin(136/2)$

which can be approximated by evaluating the sine term to give,

$A = d^2/1.8544$

where *d* is the average length of the diagonal left by the indenter in millimeters. Hence,

$HV= F/A = 1.8544\ F / d^2$

where *F* is in kgf and *d* is in millimeters.

The corresponding unit of HV is then kilograms-force per square millimeter (kgf/mm^2) or HV number. In the above equation, "F" could be in N and "d" in mm, giving HV in the SI unit of MPa. To calculate Vickers hardness number (VHN) using SI units one needs to convert the force applied from newtons to kilogram-force by dividing by 9.806 65 (standard gravity). This leads to the following equation:

$HV=F/A=0.1891\ F / d^2$

F= Load in kgf

d = Arithmetic mean of the two diagonals, $d_1$and $d_2$in mm

HV = Vickers hardness

where *F* is in N and *d* is in millimeters. A common error is that the above formula to calculate the HV number does not result in a number with the unit Newton per square millimeter (N/mm^2), but results directly in the Vickers hardness number (usually given without units), which is in fact kilograms-force per square millimeter (kgf/mm^2).

The Vickers scale ranges from 10 gf to100 kgf. For Vickers hardness testing,the obtained hardness value is relativelyunaffected by the applied load.For spacing between Vickers indents

Vickers hardness numbers are reported as **xxxHVyy**, e.g. **440HV30**, or **xxxHVyy/zz** if duration of force differs from 10 s to 15 s, e.g. 440HV30/20, where:

- **440** is the hardness number,
- **HV** gives the hardness scale (Vickers),
- **30** indicates the load used in kgf.
- **20** indicates the loading time if it differs from 10 s to 15 s

To convert the Vickers hardness number to SI units the hardness number in kilograms-force per square millimeter (kgf/mm^2) has to be multiplied with the standard gravity (9.806 65) to get the hardness in MPa (N/mm^2) and furthermore divided by 1000 to get the hardness in GPa. Vickers hardness can also be converted to an SI hardness based on the projected area of the indent rather than the surface area. The projected area,A_p {\displaystyle A_{p}}, is defined as the following for a Vickers indenter geometry

$A_p= d_{avg}{}^2/2$

This hardness is sometimes referred to as the mean contact area and ideally can be directly compared with other hardness tests also defined using projected area.

Vickers values are generally independent of the test force: they will come out the same for 500 gf and 50 kgf, as long as the force is at least 200 gf.However, lower load indents often display a dependence of hardness on indent depth known as the indentation size effect (ISE).

For thin samples indentation depth can be an issue due to substrate effects. As a rule of thumb the sample thickness should be kept greater than 2.5 times the indent diameter. Alternatively indent depth, t{\displaystyle t}, can be calculated according to:

$t = d_{avg}/ 7.0006$

If HV is first expressed in N/mm^2 (MPa), or otherwise by converting from kgf/mm^2, then the tensile strength (in MPa) of the material can be approximated as $\sigma_u \approx HV/c \approx HV/3$, where *c* is a constant determined by yield strength, Poisson's ratio, work-hardening exponent and geometrical factors – usually ranging between 2 and 4. In other words, if HV is expressed in N/mm^2 (i.e. in MPa) then the tensile strength (in MPa) ≈ HV/3. This empirical law depends variably on the work-hardening behavior of the material

Advantages

The advantages of the Vickers hardness test are that extremely accurate readings can be taken, and just one type of indenter is used for all types of metals and surface treatments. Although thoroughly adaptable and very precise for testing the softest and hardest of materials, under varying loads,Vickers is the most versatile method,due to only one indenter and many loads(micro/macro hardness range). Can beused for all materials and many applications(case hardness depth measurements,Jominy testing, welds, ceramicsand coatings), but requires a relativelygood surface finish.

Disadvantages

The Vickers machine is a floor standing unit that is more expensive than the Brinell or Rockwell machines.

Application

The fin attachment pins and sleeves in the Convair 580 airliner were specified by the aircraft manufacturer to be hardened to a Vickers Hardness specification of 390HV5, the '5' meaning five kiloponds. However, on the aircraft flying Partnair Flight 394 the pins were later found to have been replaced with sub-standard parts, leading to rapid wear and finally loss of the aircraft. On examination, accident investigators found that the sub-standard pins had a hardness value of only some 200-230HV5.

2.3. TENSILE TEST

Tensile testing, also known as **tension testing**, is a fundamental materials science and engineering test in which a sample is subjected to a controlled tension until failure. Properties that are directly measured via a tensile test are ultimate tensile strength, breaking strength, maximum elongation and reduction in area. From these measurements the following properties can also be determined: Young's modulus, Poisson's ratio, yield strength, and strain-hardening characteristics.

Concepts of Stress and Strain

To compare specimens of different sizes, the load iscalculated per unit area.

Engineering stress: $\sigma = F / A_o$

F is load applied perpendicular to specimen crosssection;

A_0 is cross-sectional area (perpendicular tothe force) **before** application of the load.

Engineering strain: $\varepsilon = \Delta l / l_o$ **(×100 %)**

Δl is change in length, lo is the original length.

These definitions of stress and strain allow one tocompare test results for specimens of different crosssectionalarea A_0 and of different length l_0. **Stress and strain are positive for tensile loads, negative for compressive loads.**

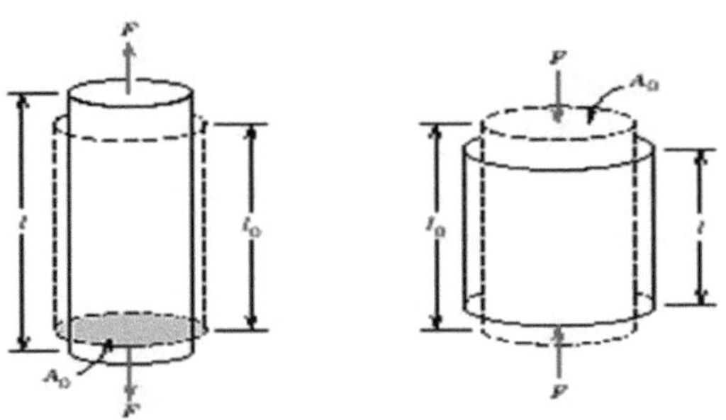

Fig. 2.12 Tensile loads and Compressive loads

Purpose of tensile testing

Tensile testing might have a variety of purposes, such as:

- Select a material or item for an application
- Predict how a material will perform in use: normal and extreme forces.
- Determine if, or verify that, the requirements of a specification, regulation, or contract are met

- Decide if a new product development program is on track
- Demonstrate proof of concept
- Demonstrate the utility of a proposed patent
- Provide standarddata for other scientific, engineering, and quality assurance functions
- Provide a basis for Technical communication
- Provide a technical means of comparison of several options
- Provide evidence in legal proceedings

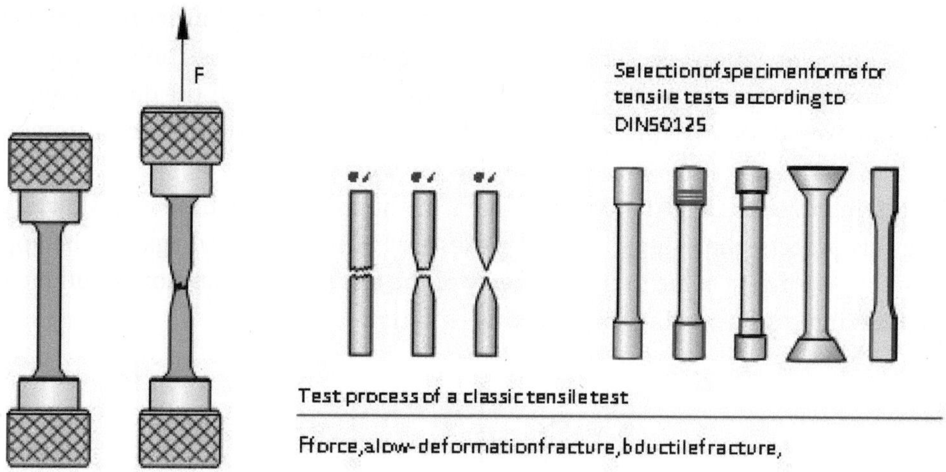

Fig. 2.13 Tensile testing

Tensile testing is most often carried out at a material testing laboratory. The ASTM D638 is among the most common tensile testing protocols. The ASTM D638 measures plastics tensile properties including ultimate tensile strength, yield strength, elongation and Poisson's ratio.

The most common testing machine used in tensile testing is the *universal testing machine*. This type of machine has two *crossheads*; one is adjusted for the length of the specimen and the other is driven to apply tension to the test specimen. There are two types: hydraulic powered and electromagnetically powered machines.

The machine must have the proper capabilities for the test specimen being tested. There are four main parameters: force capacity, speed, precision and accuracy. Force capacity refers to the fact that the machine must be able to generate enough force to fracture the specimen. The machine must be able to apply the force quickly or slowly enough to properly mimic the actual application. Finally, the machine must be able to accurately and precisely measure the gauge length and forces applied; for instance, a large machine that is designed to measure long elongations may not work with a brittle material that experiences short elongations prior to fracturing.

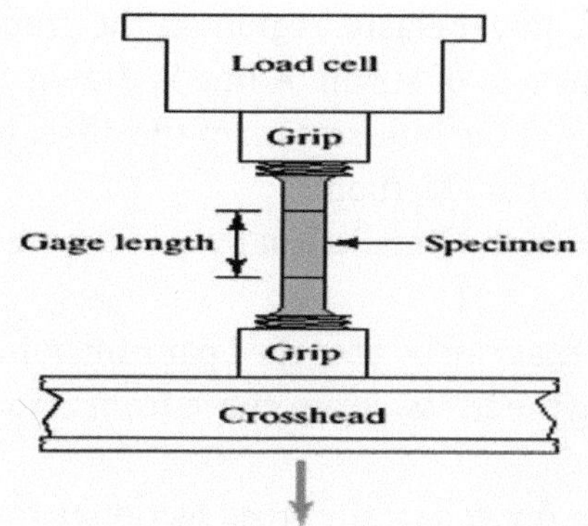

Fig. 2.14 Tensile Machine

Alignment of the test specimen in the testing machine is critical, because if the specimen is misaligned, either at an angle or offset to one side, the machine will exert a bending force on the specimen. This is especially bad for brittle materials, because it will dramatically skew the results. This situation can be minimized by using spherical seats or U-joints between the grips and the test machine.If the initial portion of the stress–strain curve is curved and not linear, it indicates the specimen is misaligned in the testing machine.

The strain measurements are most commonly measured with an extensometer, but strain gauges are also frequently used on small test specimen or when Poisson's ratio is being measured.Newer test machines have digital time, force, and elongation measurement systems consisting of electronic sensors connected to a data collection device (often a computer) and software to manipulate and output the data. However, analog machines continue to meet and exceed ASTM, NIST, and ASM metal tensile testing accuracy requirements, continuing to be used today.

The test process involves placing the test specimen in the testing machine and slowly extending it until it fractures. During this process, the elongation of the gauge section is recorded against the applied force. The data is manipulated so that it is not specific to the geometry of the test sample. The elongation measurement is used to calculate the engineering strain, ε, using the following equation

$$\%EL = \left(\frac{l_f - l_0}{l_0}\right) \times 100$$

$$\%RA = \left(\frac{A_0 - A_f}{A_0}\right) \times 100$$

The Elastic Modulus or Young's Modulus is determined by the ratio of stress to strain below the elastic limit. The Modulus of Elasticity measures the stiffness of a material but it only applies to the portion of the test where the ratio of stress to strain is constant. On an *x/y* axis graph of the Tensile Test this portion of the test would be represented by the straight line portion of the graph prior to the beginning of the curve. At this point in the test, if the load were to be removed, the test specimen would return to its original condition. After this point in the test, plastic deformation begins to occur, and the test specimen will not return to its original proportions upon relaxation of the load.

The Offset Method for determining Yield Strength is used when the material being tested does not show an easily identifiable departure point from the linear elastic region on the graph. Many metals and most plastics fall into this category. An offset is specified as a % of strain. A line is drawn from the offset with the same slope as the Modulus of Elasticity. The stress value at the intersection of the offset line with the line of the linear elastic region is then used for the Yield Strength by Offset Method.

Modulus of Toughness is determined in the Tensile Test by calculating the total area under the stress/strain curve to the point of failure.

Modulus of Resilience is the energy that can be absorbed per unit volume without causing permanent distortion. And may be calculated by integrating the stress/strain curve from zero to the elastic limit and then dividing by the original volume.

Fracture Stress is the load at fracture divided by the cross sectional area at fracture.

Engineering Stress and Strain is the ratio of the applied load to the undeformed cross-sectional area, while, True

Stress and Strain is the ratio of the applied force to the instantaneous cross-sectional area. True Stress and Strain calculates for the reduced area of the test specimen as plastic deformation occurs. For most applications involving small strain rates (less than 5%) Engineering Stress and Strain are accurate enough. For larger strain rates, the more involved calculations to arrive at True Stress and Strain become necessary.

2.4. IMPACT TEST

Impact is a very important phenomenon in governing the life of a structure. For example, in the case of an aircraft, impact can take place by a bird hitting a plane while it is cruising, or during take off and landing the aircraft may be struck by debris that is present on the runway, and as well as other causes. It must also be calculated for roads if speed breakers are present, in bridge construction where vehicles punch an impact load, etc.

In mechanics, an **impact** is a high force or shock applied over a short time period when two or more bodies collide. Such a force or acceleration usually has a greater effect than a lower force applied over a proportionally longer period. The effect depends critically on the relative velocity of the bodies to one another.

A mechanical or physical **shock** is a sudden acceleration caused, for example, by impact, drop, kick, earthquake, or explosion. Shock is a transient physical excitation.

Shock describes matter subject to extreme rates of force with respect to time. Shock is a vector that has units of an acceleration (rate of change of velocity). The unit *g* (or **g**) represents multiples of the acceleration of gravity and is conventionally used.

A shock pulse can be characterised by its peak acceleration, the duration, and the shape of the shock pulse (half sine, triangular, trapezoidal, etc.). The Shock response spectrum is a method for further evaluating a mechanical shock.

Impact tests are used in studying the toughness of material. A material's toughness is a factor of its ability to absorb energy during plastic deformation. Brittle materials have low toughness as a result of the small amount of plastic deformation they can endure. The impact value of a material can also change with temperature. Generally, at lower temperatures, the impact energy of a material is decreased.Both Charpy and Izod impact testing are popular methods of determining impact strength, or toughness, of a material. In other words, these tests measure the total amount of energy that a material is able to absorb. This energy absorption is directly related to the brittleness of the material. Brittle materials, such as ceramics or glass, tend to have lower absorption rates than ductile materials like copper or aluminum.

Understanding a material's energy absorption properties is critical, as it predicts how much plastic deformation the material will be able to withstand before catastrophic failure. It is also important to understand the similarities and differences between these two common impact test methods.

The Charpy and Izod tests are two well-known methods for studying the toughness of materials. Many industries use either of the two for testing material strength. The tests measure the amount of energy absorbed by a notched sample when it gets hit by a weighted pendulum. The computed energy serves as a measure of the specimen's toughness.

Testers use a pendulum impact testing machine to perform the Charpy or the Izod impact test.

The Charpy impact test is still one of the most popular impact test methods. The main reason for this is because samples for the test are easy to prepare. Results are also very easy to compute.The equipment for the Izod impact and Charpy tester are almost identical. But, there are differences such as the orientation of the material in the impact tester. While both the Izod and Charpy methods measure similar properties, the specimen design and testing configuration are different enough that care should be taken when choosing with method to perform. Your testing provider should be able to provide method recommendations based on your end goals and specific material in question.

Westmoreland Mechanical Testing & Research also offers a line of Instrumented Impact Testing designed to simulate real life rapid energy absorption conditions caused by: falling objects, blows, collisions, drops, etc.

2.4.1 CHARPY IMPACT TESTING

The test was developed around 1900 by S. B. Russell (1898, American) and Georges Charpy (1901, French). The test became known as the Charpy test in the early 1900s due to the technical contributions and standardization efforts by Charpy.

In 1896, S. B. Russell introduced the idea of *residual fracture energy* and devised a pendulum fracture test. Russell's initial tests measured un-notched samples. In 1897, Frémont introduced a test to measure the same phenomenon using a spring-loaded machine. In 1901, Georges Charpy proposed a standardized method improving Russell's by introducing a redesigned pendulum and notched sample, giving precise specifications.

The **Charpy impact test**, also known as the **Charpy V-notch test**, is a standardized high strain-rate test which determines the amount of energy absorbed by a material during fracture. Absorbed energy is a measure of the material's notchtoughness. It is widely used in industry, since it is easy to prepare and conduct and results can be obtained quickly and cheaply. A disadvantage is that some results are only comparative. The test was pivotal in understanding the fracture problems of ships during World War II.

4.1.1 Procedure and principle of test

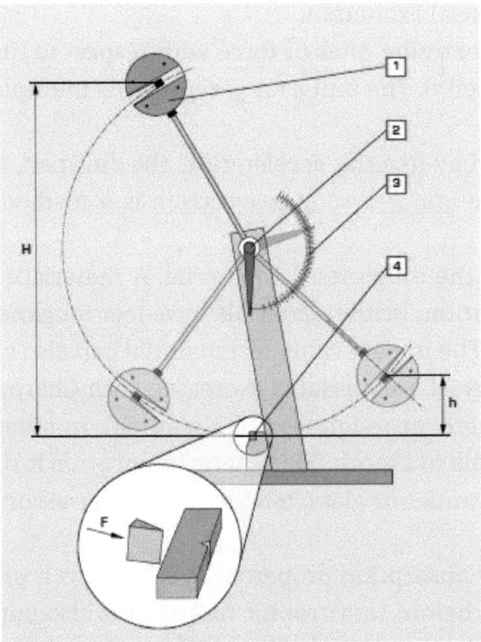

Fig. 2.15 Pendulum impact testing machine

A pendulum impact testing machine or a pendulum impact tester is an apparatus with a swinging pendulum that gets released to impact a secured specimen. The pendulum has a weighted hammer at its end, which hits the sample material.

Specimens for impact testing can be metals, metallic alloys, or plastic materials.The specimen will either have a V or a U shaped notch in it. Specimens may get deformed if there are no notches in them. There may also be inconsistencies in the test results when there are no notches in the material.

Testers use a broaching machine or a notch cutter to make the notches on the sample material. The depth for a V shaped notch is 2mm deep and 5mm deep for a U shaped notched specimen.

Materials are often heated up or cooled down before testing. This is for testing specimens exposed at different temperatures. The specimens may undergo a series of tests at specific temperatures. Sometimes, test results are the average of five specimens.

To perform the impact test, the operator first raises and locks the pendulum at a fixed height. The tester then places the specimen on a support in the striking anvil. Tester makes sure that the specimen is well secured.

An indicator or dial is then reset. After some safety checks, the tester releases the pendulum to impact the specimen. The tester can use a heavier hammer if there is no breakage.

After impact, the tester computes the energy absorbed by the material. This is the difference between the height of the pendulum at the start and its height after the impact blow.

The apparatus consists of a pendulum of known mass and length that is dropped from a known height to impact a notched specimen of material. The energy transferred to the material can be inferred by comparing the difference in the height of the hammer before and after the fracture (energy absorbed by the fracture event).It remains to this day one of the most popular impact testing methods due to the relative ease of creating samples and obtaining results. The test apparatus consists of a weighted pendulum, which is dropped from a specified height to make contact with the specimen. The energy transferred to the material can be inferred by comparing the difference in the height of the pendulum before and after the fracture.

The notch in the sample affects the results of the impact test, thus it is necessary for the notch to be of regular dimensions and geometry. The size of the sample can also affect results, since the dimensions determine whether or not the material is in plane strain. This difference can greatly affect the conclusions made.

A Charpy test specimen, which is placed horizontally into the machine, is typically a 55 x 10 x 10mm (2.165" x 0.394" x 0.394") bar with a notch machined into one of the faces. This notch, which can be either V-shaped or U-shaped, is placed facing away from the pendulum and helps to concentrate the stress and encourage fracture. Testing can be performed at both ambient and reduced temperatures, sometimes as low as -425F.

The *Standard methods for Notched Bar Impact Testing of Metallic Materials* can be found in ASTM E23, ISO 148-1 or EN 10045-1 (retired and replaced with ISO 148-1),where all the aspects of the test and equipment used are described in detail

The quantitative result of the impact tests the energy needed to fracture a material and can be used to measure the toughness of the material. There is a connection to the yield strength but it cannot be expressed by a standard formula. Also, the strain rate may be studied and analyzed for its effect on fracture.

The ductile-brittle transition temperature (DBTT) may be derived from the temperature where the energy needed to fracture the material drastically changes. However, in practice there is no sharp transition and it is difficult to obtain a precise transition temperature (it is really a transition region). An exact DBTT may be empirically derived in many ways: a specific absorbed energy, change in aspect of fracture (such as 50% of the area is cleavage), etc.

The qualitative results of the impact test can be used to determine the ductility of a material. If the material breaks on a flat plane, the fracture was brittle, and if the material breaks with jagged edges or shear lips, then the fracture was ductile. Usually, a material does not break in just one way or the other and thus comparing the jagged to flat surface areas of the fracture will give an estimate of the percentage of ductile and brittle fracture

Charpy impact testing is most commonly performed to ASTM E23, ASTM A370, ISO 148, or EN 10045-1. While the test is most commonly performed on metals, there are also a number of standards that exist for plastics and polymers, including ASTM D6110 and ISO 179.

According to ASTM A370, the standard specimen size for Charpy impact testing is 10 mm × 10 mm × 55 mm. Subsize specimen sizes are: 10 mm × 7.5 mm × 55 mm, 10 mm × 6.7 mm × 55 mm, 10 mm × 5 mm × 55 mm, 10 mm × 3.3 mm × 55 mm, 10 mm × 2.5 mm × 55 mm. Details of specimens as per ASTM A370 (Standard Test Method and Definitions for Mechanical Testing of Steel Products).

According to EN 10045-1 (retired and replaced with ISO 148),standard specimen sizes are 10 mm × 10 mm × 55 mm. Subsize specimens are: 10 mm × 7.5 mm × 55 mm and 10 mm × 5 mm × 55 mm.

According to ISO 148, standard specimen sizes are 10 mm × 10 mm × 55 mm. Subsize specimens are: 10 mm × 7.5 mm × 55 mm, 10 mm × 5 mm × 55 mm and 10 mm × 2.5 mm × 55 mm.

According to MPIF Standard 40, the standard unnotched specimen size is 10 mm (±0.125 mm) x 10 mm (±0.125 mm) x 55 mm (±2.5 mm).

Impact test results on low- and high-strength materials

The impact energy of low-strength metals that do not show a change of fracture mode with temperature, is usually high and insensitive to temperature. For these reasons, impact tests are not widely used for assessing the fracture-resistance of low-strength materials whose fracture modes remain unchanged with temperature. Impact tests typically show a ductile-brittle transition for low-strength materials that do exhibit change in fracture mode with temperature such as body-centered cubic (BCC) transition metals.

Generally, high-strength materials have low impact energies which attest to the fact that fractures easily initiate and propagate in high-strength materials. The impact energies of high-strength materials other than steels or BCC transition metals are usually insensitive to temperature. High-strength BCC steels display a wider variation of impact energy than high-strength metal that do not have a BCC structure because steels undergo microscopic ductile-brittle transition. Regardless, the maximum impact energy of high-strength steels is still low due to their brittleness.

2.4.2 IZOD IMPACT TESTING

Impact tests are used in studying the toughness of material. A material's toughness is a factor of its ability to absorb energy during plastic deformation. Brittle materials have low toughness as a result of the small amount of plastic deformation they can endure. The impact value of a material can also change with temperature. Generally, at lower temperatures, the impact energy of a material is decreased. The size of the specimen may also affect the value of the Izod impact test because it may allow a different number of imperfections in the material, which can act as stress risers and lower the impact energy.The size of the specimen may also affect the value of the Izod impact test because it may allow a different number of imperfections in the material, which can act as stress risers and lower the impact energy.

The **Izod impact strength test** is an ASTM standard method of determining the impact resistance of materials. A pivoting arm is raised to a specific height (constant potential energy) and then released. The arm swings down hitting a notched sample, breaking the specimen. The energy absorbed by the sample is calculated from the height the arm swings to after hitting the sample. A notched sample is generally used to determine impact energy and notch sensitivity.

The test is similar to the Charpy impact test but uses a different arrangement of the specimen under test.TheIzod impact test differs from the Charpy impact test in that the sample is held in a cantilevered beam configuration as opposed to a three-point bending configuration.to perform Izod impact, you will need to decide on which specimen configuration to use. There are varying configurations of round specimens versus square specimens and single notched specimens versus those with up to three notches. Since it is often required to average 3 results for impact testing, the 3 notch specimen could be more economical, as it will take less material to get three impact results. Another possible advantage of the 3 notch sample is that the final result can be an average of directions depending on the specimen configuration. This could help eliminate bias caused by directional properties if this is a concern for your material.

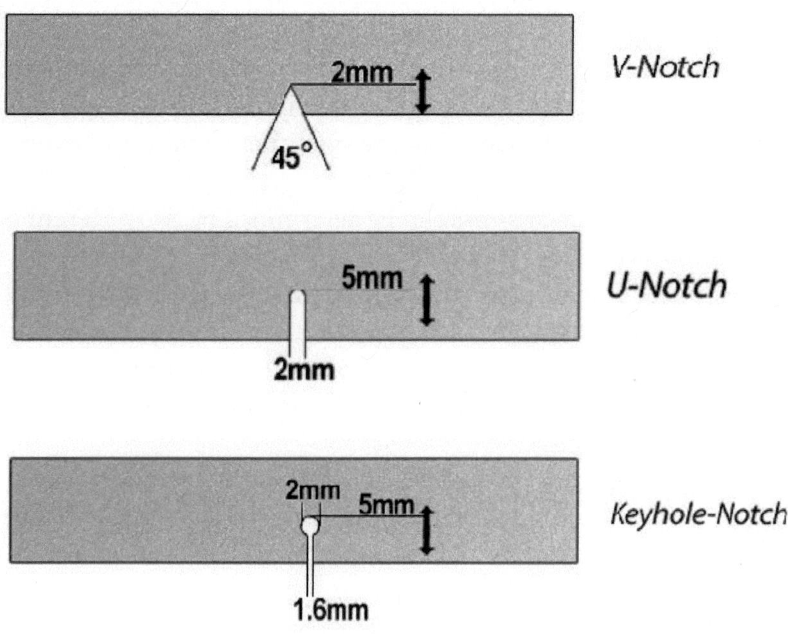

Fig. 2.16 Izod Impact Test

2.6. ***SHEAR TEST***

A shear test is designed to ap*ply stress to a test sample so that it experiences a sliding failure along a plane that is parallel to the forces applied. Generally, shear forces cause one surface of a material to move in one direction and the other surface to move in the opposite direction so that the material is stressed in a sliding motion. Shear tests differ from tension and compression tests in that the forces applied are parallel to the two contact surface, whereas, in tension and compression they are perpendicular to the contact surfaces.Shear testing is different from tensile and compression testing in that the forces applied are parallel to the upper and lower faces of the object under test. Materials behave differently in shear than in tension or compression, resulting in different values for strength and stiffness. Usually performed on fasteners, such as bolts, machine screws and rivets, shear testing applies a lateral shear force to the specimen until failure results.

Lap shear testing is performed to determine the shear strength of an adhesive that is applied to two metal plates and pulled to failure. It can be used to compare between adhesive types or different lots within the same adhesive.

Purpose of shear testing:

The most common use of a shear test is to determine the shear strength, which is the maximum shear stress that the material can withstand before failure occurs, of a material. This is a very important design characteristic of many types of fasteners such as bolts and screws. For example, when a bolt is used to secure two plates together it will experience a shear forces if the plates themselves experience any forces parallel to their plane that attempt to separate them. If the small fastener fails in shear it may lead to a chain of failures that could lead to the entire destruction of a much larger structure

Types of shear tests:

Generally there are two common types of shear tests. The first requires that the sample be setup in a modified three point flexure or four point bend fixture. The purpose of this test is to load the sample so that it experiences double shear or so that the sample has two locations where the forces are applied. Each end of the sample is anchored and the force is applied over the middle of the sample in an attempt to remove the midsection so that both ends are left behind. The second test requires that the sample have tapered ends that are each placed into grip fixtures that have been offset from the vertical axis of the sample. The sample is then pulled so that the opposite faces are pulled in opposing directions.

Shear test to study the load capacity against shearing.The shear test is applied when testing screws, rivets, pins and parallel keys in order to determine the shear strength of the material or the Behaviour of the material under shear strain. To do this, the shear stresses are produced in the specimen by means of external shear forces until the specimen shears off.

The resistance of a material against the shear stress can be determined by two different methods, the single-shear and the double-shear testing method.

In the double-shear method, the specimen is sheared off at two cross sections. In the single-shear process, the specimen only shears away at one cross section. Calculating the shear strength in the two processes differs in the cross-sectional area to be applied. The shear strength determined in the shear test is important in the design of bolts, rivets and pins, as well as for calculating the force required for shears and presses.

Shear strength in the double-shear method

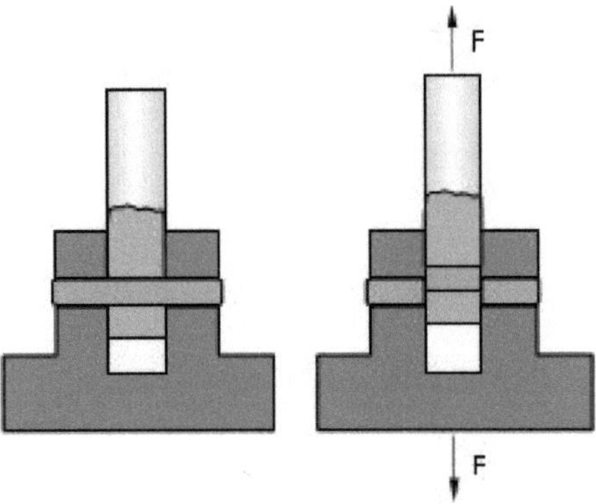

Fig. 2.16 Shear strength Test

Shear strength measures a material's ability to resist forces that cause the material to slide against itself. Popular methods of testing include Single lap shear (bevelled& joggled), Double lap she involve testing a material that has been glued together. A universal test machine is used to apply the tensile or compressive load to determine ar, and Double-butt lap shear. A common shear test would the overall strength of the adhesive once the samples are pulled or pushed apart. Shear testing is not limited to adhesives but can also be applied to samples that have been welded together, for example, or joined in any number of ways

2.7. BEND TEST

Bend tests for ductility provide a simple way to evaluate the quality of materials by their ability to resist cracking or other surface irregularities during one continuous bend. No reversal of the bend force shall be employed when conducting these tests.

Bend tests are conducted to determine the ductility or strength of a material. The types of bend tests discussed are bending ductility tests, bending strength tests (ASTM E 855), bend tests as per EN 12384 and JIS 3130, and computer-aided bending tests. The three standard bending strength tests are the cantilever beam bend test, the three-point bend test, and the four-point bend test.

The type of bend test used determines the location of the forces and constraints on the bent portion of the specimen, ranging from no direct contact to continuous contact.

The test can terminate at a given angle of bend over a specified radius or continue until the specimen legs are in contact. The bend angle can be measured while the specimen is under the bending force (usually when the semi-guided bend test is employed), or after removal of the force as when performing a free-bend test. Product requirements for the material being tested determine the method used.

Materials with an as-fabricated cross section of rectangular, round, hexagonal, or similar defined shape can be tested in full section to evaluate their bend properties by using the procedures outlined in these test methods, in which case relative width and thickness requirements do not apply.

Principle & procedure for bending test

These test methods cover bend testing for ductility of materials. Included in the procedures are four conditions of constraint on the bent portion of the specimen; a guided-bend test using a mandrel or plunger of defined dimensions to force the mid-length of the specimen between two supports separated by a defined space; a semi-guided bend test in which the specimen is bent, while in contact with a mandrel, through a specified angle or to a specified inside radius (r) of curvature, measured while under the bending force; a free-bend test in which the ends of the specimen are brought toward each other, but in which no transverse force is applied to the bend itself and there is no contact of the concave inside surface of the bend with other material; a bend and flatten test, in which a transverse force is applied to the bend such that the legs make contact with each other over the length of the specimen.

After bending, the convex surface of the bend is examined for evidence of a crack or surface irregularities. If the specimen fractures, the material has failed the test. When complete fracture does not occur, the criterion for failure is the number and size of cracks or surface irregularities visible to the unaided eye occurring on the convex surface of the specimen after bending, as specified by the product standard. Any cracks within one thickness of the edge of the specimen are not considered a bend test failure. Cracks occurring in the corners of the bent portion shall not be considered significant unless they exceed the size specified for corner cracks in the product standard.

The values stated in SI units are to be regarded as standard. Inch-pound values given in parentheses were used in establishing test parameters and are for information only.

The bend test consists of submitting a test. piece of round, square,rectangular, or polygonal cross section to plastic deformation by bending,without changing the direction of loading, until a specified angle of bendis reached.

The axes of the two legs of the test piece remain in a planeperpendicular to the axis of bending. In the case of 130' bend, the twolateral surfaces may, depending on the requirements of the material.standard, lie flat against each other or may be parallel at a specifieddistance, an insert being used to control this distance.

In general, the test is carried out at ambient temperature between 10 and 35%. Tests carried out under controlled conditions shall be made at a temperature of 23 f 5°C. 6.2.

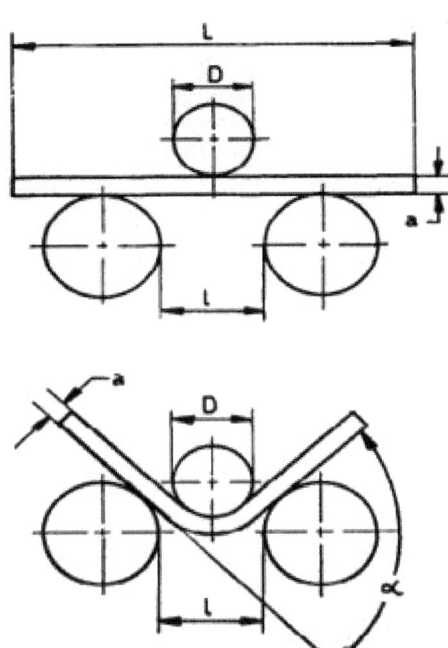

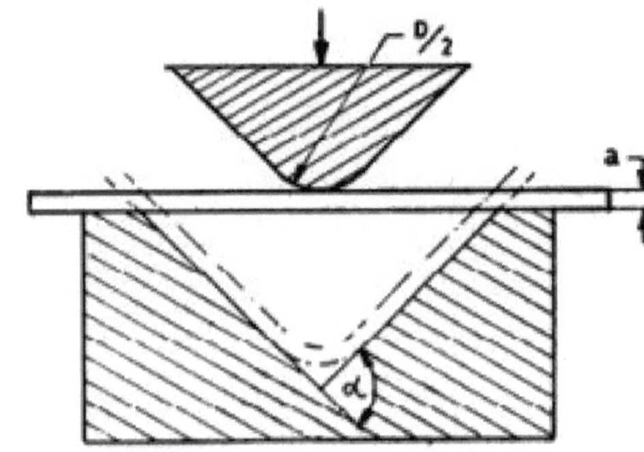

Fig. 2 Bend Test by the Use of V-Block

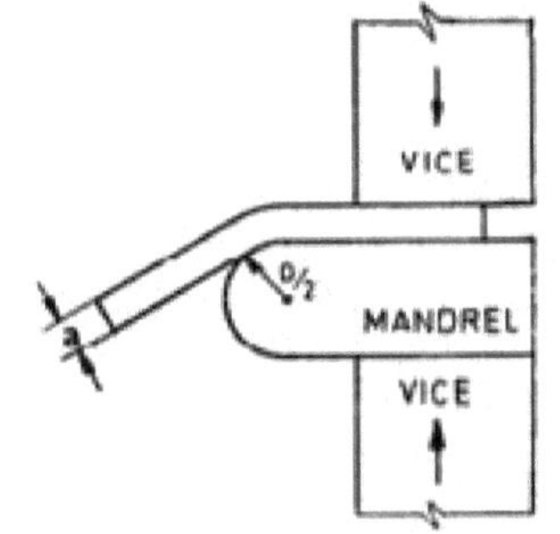

Fig. 1 Simple Bend Test

Fig. 3 Bend Test Through an Angle Over a Specified Radius'

Fig. 2.17 Shear Test

Advantages

The bend test is a simple and inexpensive qualitative test that can be used to evaluate both the ductility and soundness of a material. It is often used as a quality control test for butt-welded joints, having the advantage of simplicity of both test piece and equipment.

No expensive test equipment is needed, test specimens are easily prepared and the test can, if required, be carried out on the shop floor as a quality control test to ensure consistency in production.

The bend test uses a coupon that is bent in three point bending to a specified angle.The outside of the bend is extensively plastically deformed so that any defects in, or embrittlement of, the material will be revealed by the premature failure of the coupon.

2.8. Creep Test

Creep is a property of great importance in materials used for high-temperature applications. It may be defined as a continuing slow plastic flow under constant conditions of load or stress. Materials are often placed in service at relatively high temperatures and exposed to static mechanical stresses. These stresses are less than the yield strength of the material but nevertheless can cause plastic deformation to take place particularly over a long period of service time. This phenomenon is known as creep. Due to creep, rate of deformation continues with time under stresses well below the yield strength for the particular temperature to which the metal is subjected. Materials behave differently under lasting static loads at increased temperatures than they do under the same load at room temperature. After a certain amount of time, increased temperatures under stresses below the hot yield point and without an increase in load lead to a slow but steady irreversible plastic deformation, also known as creep. After a sufficiently long, even load time, this leads to fracture of the specimen.

Creep curve If the elongation is plotted over time, we get the creep curve.

Figure given below shows how in general the strength and hardness of a metal varies with temperature. T_m is the melting temperature of the material. The temperature is measured on the Kelvin scale, whose origin is absolute zero

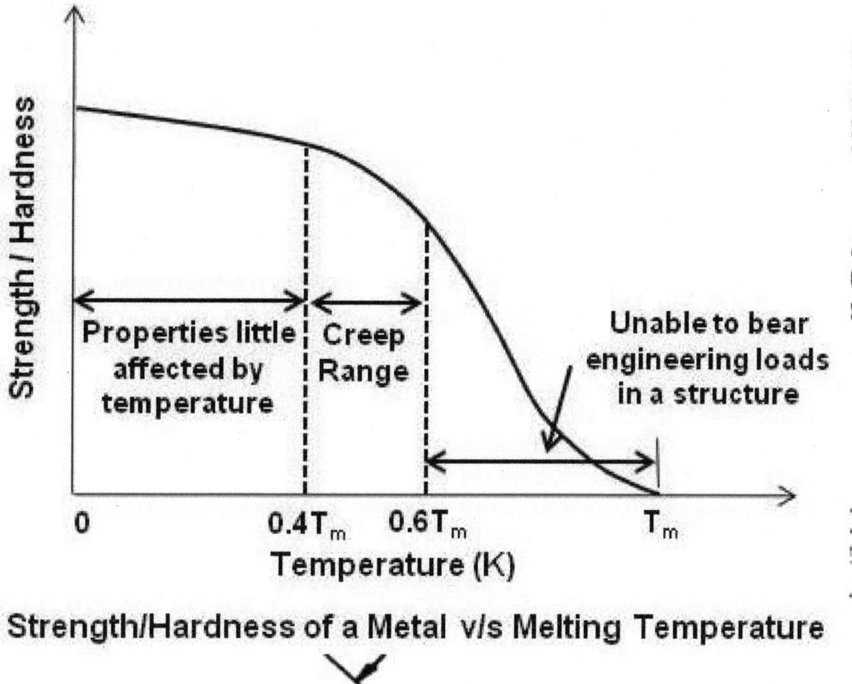

Fig. 2.18 Strength and Temperath

Figure given below shows the effect of temperature on creep strain.

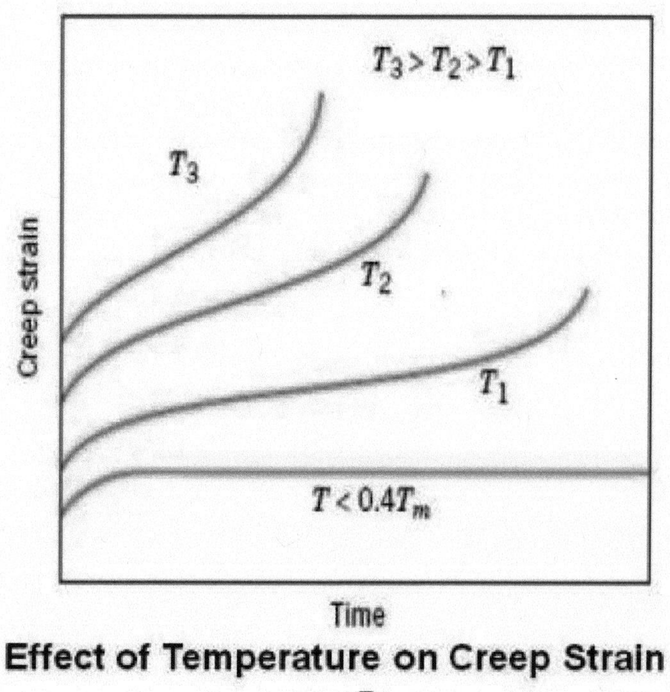

Fig. 2.18 relation Between Creep and Temperature

Creep is observed in all material types it ony becomes important at temperatures greater than about 0.4T_m (where T_m is the melting point in Kelvin). Soft metals such as tin and lead creep at room temperature while aluminium and its alloys creep at around 250Â°C. Steel creeps at about 450Â°C while nickel-based alloys (nimonics) creep at around 650Â°C

Design of Components for Creep

The temperature and length of service determines whether or not creep must be considered as a possible mode of failure for a given material component. For example one particular aluminium-copper alloy was used for the forged impellers in the jet engine for an aircraft. In this application, the temperature of operation was up to 200Â°C and the stress was high enough to limit the life to a few hundred hours. Clearly, in this case, 200Â°C is a creep-producing temperature. The same alloy is used as the skin for Concorde (aircraft), and over most of this structure the temperature does not exceed 120Â°C. However, the Concorde airframe is designed for a life in service of 20,000â€“30,000 hours, and this is a long enough period for 120Â°C to constitute a possible hazard. Creep is thus important in both applications, even though the temperatures are different.

Disadvantages

Over a long period of time components elongate due to creep and may eventually become larger than designed values. This may result in insufficient running clearances for an application. Corrective action shall be taken in such cases.

Standards

ASTM E139-11(2018), Standard Test Methods for Conducting Creep, Creep-Rupture, and Stress-Rupture Tests of Metallic Materials

Applications

Creep is high temperature progressive deformation at constant stress. "High temperature" is a relative term dependent upon the materials involved. Creep rates are used in evaluating materials for boilers, gas turbines, jet engines, ovens, or any application that involves high temperatures under load. Understanding high temperature behavior of metals is useful in designing failure resistant systems. Creep testing has three different applications in the industry:

1. Displacement-Limited applications : the size must be precise and there must be little errors or tendency to change.This is most commonly found in turbine rotors in jet engines.
2. Rupture Limited applications: in this application the break cannot occur to the material but there can be various dimensions as the material goes through creep. High pressure tubes are examples of them.
3. Stress relaxation limited application : the tension at the beginning becomes more relaxed and the tension will continue to relax as the time goes by, such as cable wires and bolts.

THREE

NON DESTRUCTIVE TESTING

3.1 Nondestructive Testing (NDT)

Also known as nondestructive examination (NDE) Involves inspection and analysis of machinery or components without affecting the operation or the properties of the subject. (As opposed to a tensile test or other destructive test such as sectioning.)

3.1.1 What Is Nondestructive Testing?

Nondestructive testing asks "Is there something wrong with this material?" Nondestructive testing (NDT) has been defined as ... "those test methods used to examine an object, material or system without impairing its future usefulness."

3.1.2 The British View (BINDT)

"Non-destructive testing is the branch of engineering concerned with all methods of detecting and evaluating flaws in materials." "The essential feature of NDT is that the test process itself produces no deleterious effects on the material or structure under test."

3.1.3 A Brief History

Formal NDE dates back to early railroad days when a mixture of oil and talc were used to detect cracking in axles and wheels. Since then science has developed a wide range of tools and abilities to non invasively detect problems before they become disasters.

3.2 Visual Inspection

Visual Inspection, or Visual Testing (VT), is the oldest and most basic method of inspection. It is the process of looking over a piece of equipment using the naked eye to look for flaws. It requires no equipment except the naked eye of a trained inspector. Visual inspection can be used for internal and external surface inspection of a variety of equipment types, including storage tanks, pressure vessels, piping, and other equipment. Visual Inspection means the spection of equipment and structures using a combination of human senses such as vision, hearing, touch and smell. Visual Inspection is sometimes carried out in conjunction with devices such as a low power magnifying glass, boroscopes, fiberscopes, digital video borescopes, camera systems and robotic crawler systems.

3.2.1 Tools used in Visual Inspection

- Mirrors
- Magnifying Glasses
- Microscopes
- Borescope
- Endoscope
- Flexible fibres
- Closed circuit Television system
- Computer enhanced systems

3.2.2 Applications of Visual Inspection

- It is used to inspect whether there is a misalignment of parts in the equipment
- It checks for corrosion, erosion, cracks and deformities of machine components
- It inspect the plant components for any leakage or abnormal operation
- It is used to identify the defects in weldments

3.2.3 Limitations of Visual Inspections

- Can identify only large discontinuities
- Limited to surface discontinuities Skilled labour required
- Result depend on the eye resolution of the inspector
- It may cause eye fatigue to the inspector

3.2.4 Lighting and Lighting source

- The amount of light is depend up on the type of test.
- For an appropriate visual inspection, suitable lighting of about 800-1000 Lux
- The major lighting sources are

- Incandescent Lamp
-Fluorescent lamp
-High intensity discharge lamp

Material factors that affect Visual Testing

- Surface Condition
  - Cleanliness
  - Colour
  - Texture
- Physical Conditions
  - Specimen Condition
  - Shape and Size
  - Temperature
- Environmental Factors
  - Atmosphere
  - Cleanliness
  - Humidity and Temperature
  - Safety
- Physiological Factors
  - Physical Comfort
  - Health , mental attitude, fatigue and test item position

3.3 Types Of Visual Inspection

- Unaided visual inspection-inspection without use of any optical or mechanical instruments
- Aided Visual Inspection-Inspection with use of any optical or mechanical instruments

3.3.1 Unaided Visual Inspecton

- When a inspection of speciment or part is carried without the use of any opto-electrical or electronics devices is calles UNAIDED VISUAL INSPECTION

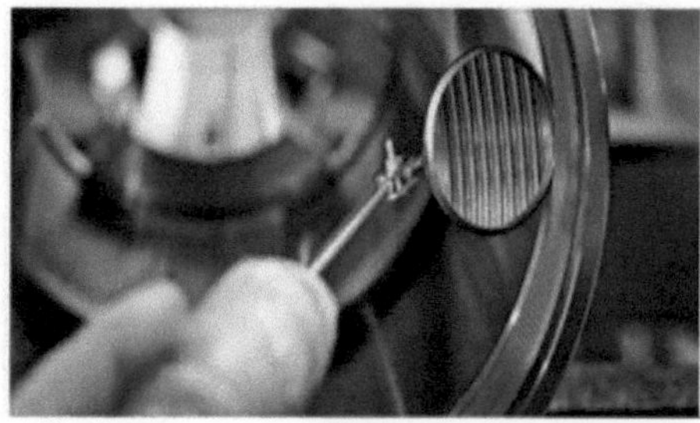
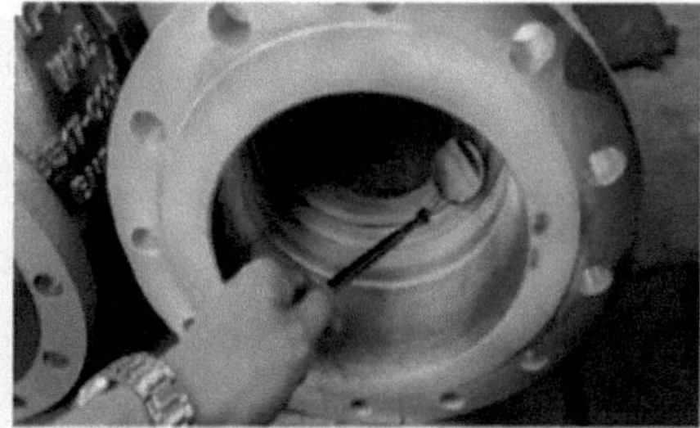

Fig 1. Unaided Visual Inspecton

- It is also known as direct visualinspection
- It can be accomplished with the help of naked eye
- It can done without the help of optical aids
- Defects can be detected are
- -Absense of cracks, Corrosion Layer, Surface porpsity, Misalignment of mated parts

3.3.2 Aided Visual Inspection

Optical Aids	Mechanical Aids
1.Microscopes	1.Micrometers
2.Borescopes	2.Calipers
3.Fiberscopes	3.Depth gauges
4.Video Cameras	4.Thread pitch gauges
	5.Feeler gauges
	6.Weld gauges

Borescope

Fig 2. Borescope

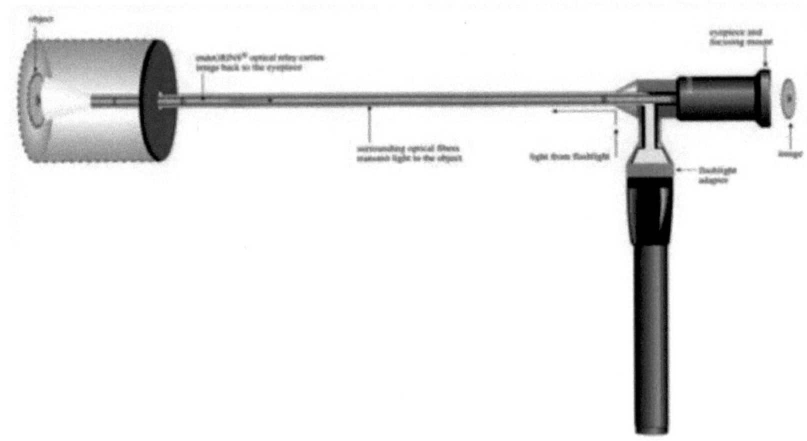

Fig 3. Borescope

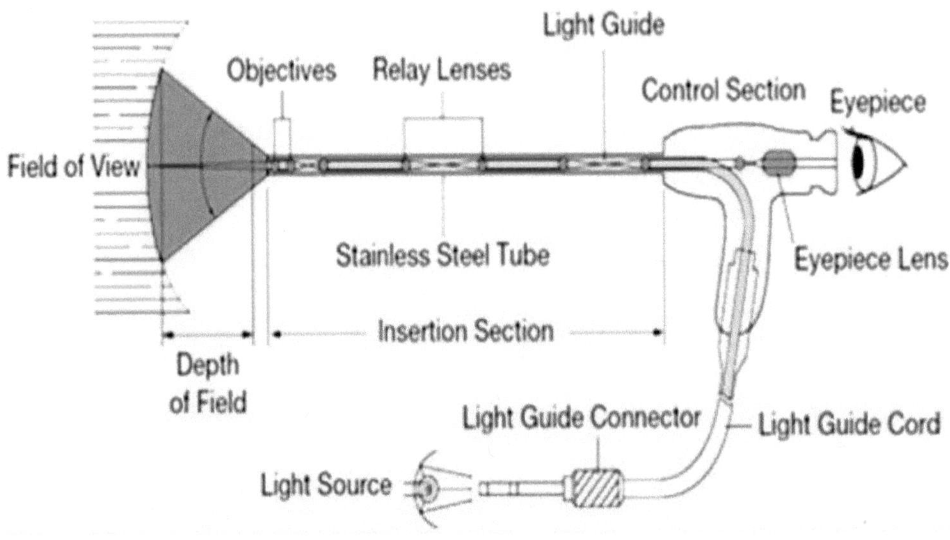

Fig 4. Borescope

Borescopes

1. A borescope is an optical device consisting of a rigid or flexible tube with an eyepiece on one end, an objective lens on the other linked together by a relay optical system in between.
2. The optical system in some instances is surrounded by optical fibers used for illumination of the remote object.
3. An internal image of the illuminated object is formed by the objective lens and magnified by the eyepiece which presents it to the viewer's eye.

Fiberscopes

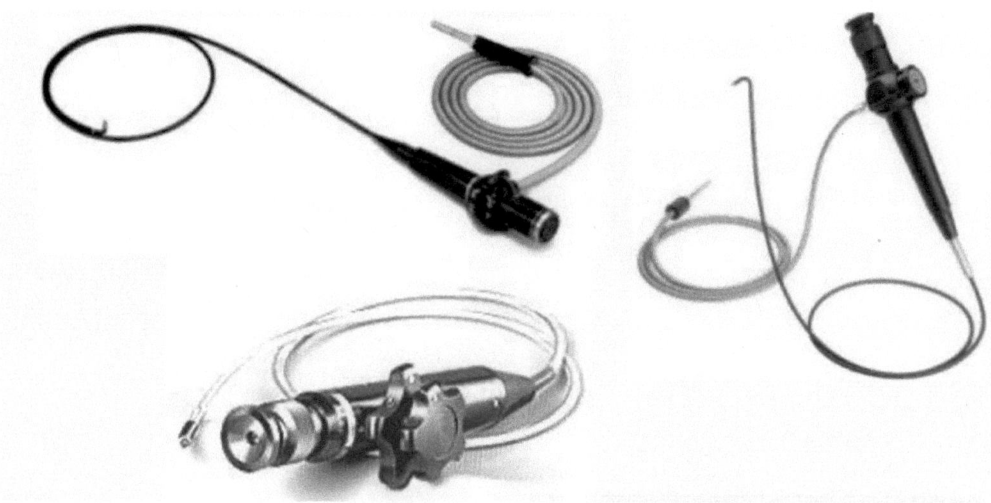

Fig 5. Fiberscopes

Video Cameras

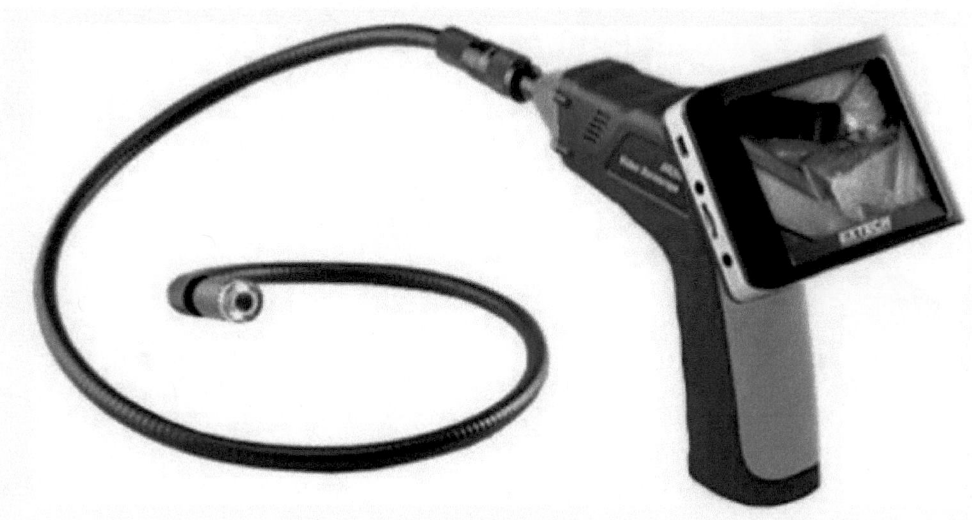

Fig 6. Video Camera

Feeler Gauges

1. A feeler gauge is a tool used to measure gap widths.
2. Feeler gauges are mostly used in engineering to measure the clearance between two parts.

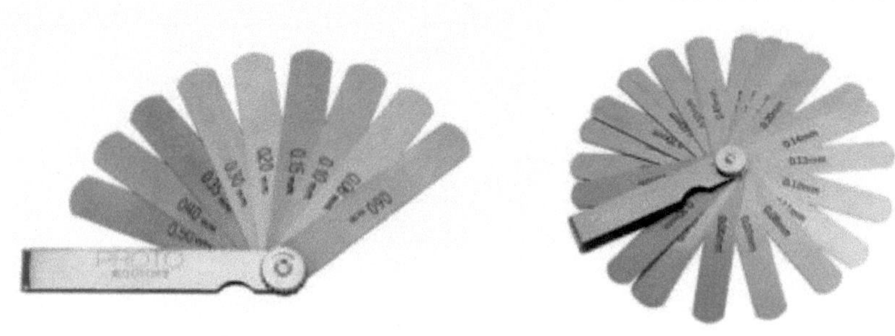

Fig 7. Feeler Gauges

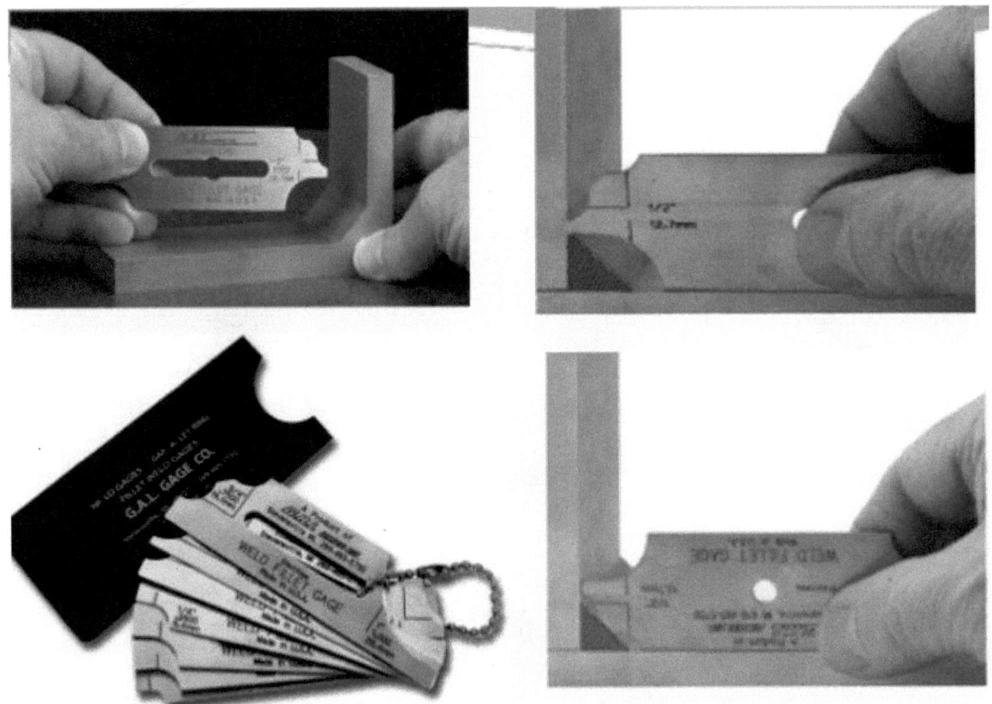

Fig 8. Feeler Gauge

3.4Liquid Penetrant Testing

Liquid penetrant inspection is one of the oldest and most widely used non destructive testing methods. It is also called as dye penetrant inspection.

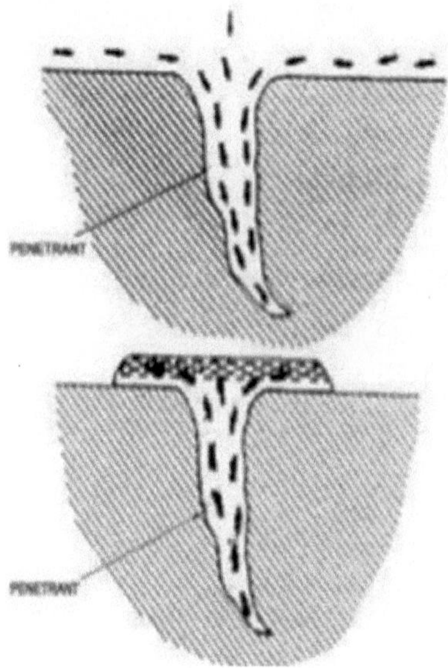

Fig 9. Liquid Penetrant Testing

- Penetrant testing can be applied to most of materials including metallic and non metallic objects
- Metallic materials include aluminum, magnesium, titanium, cast iron,
- stainless steel, powdered metal products, copper, brass, bronze, etc.
- Non metallic materials include ceramics, plastic, molded rubber, composites, glass, etc.
- Penetrant testing can't be applied on a porous surface

Penetrant Testing History

- Penetrant first used in 1900s to detect cracks in locomotive parts
- The method was called oil and whiting The method used dirty lubricating oil that was thinned with kerosene followed
- by application of chalk coating which absorbed oil from the cracks In 1940s fluorescent or visible dye was added to the oil

Penetrants

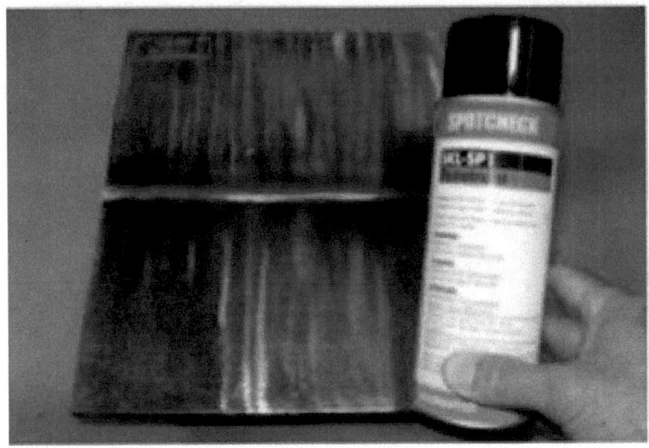

Fig 10. Penetrants

The penetrants are mixtures of organic solvents, which are characterized their ability to wet materials, spread rapidly and penetrate into minute.

Developer

Fig 11. Developer

Developer is good absorbent material capable of drawing traces trapped penetrants from the discontinues back into surfaces. It also provide a light background to increase contrast when visual penetrant is used

Steps of Liquid Penetrant Testing

The exact procedure for liquid penetrant testing can vary from case to case depending on several factors such as

- the penetrant system being used,
- the size and material of the component being inspected.
- the type of discontinuities being expected in the component
- and the condition and environment under which the inspection is performed.

Principles

- Clean & dry test object
- Apply penetrant and let it penetrate
- Remove excess penetrant
- Apply developer

- Evaluate indications
- Post clean test object

Surface Preparation:

One of the most critical steps of a liquid penetrant testing is the surface preparation. The surface must be free of oil, grease, water, or other contaminants that may prevent penetrant from entering flaws. The sample may also require etching if mechanical operations such as machining, sanding, or grit blasting have been performed. These and other mechanical operations can smear metal over the flaw opening and prevent the penetrant from entering.

Penetrant Application:

Once the surface has been thoroughly cleaned and dried, the penetrant material is applied by spraying, brushing, or immersing the part in a penetrant bath.

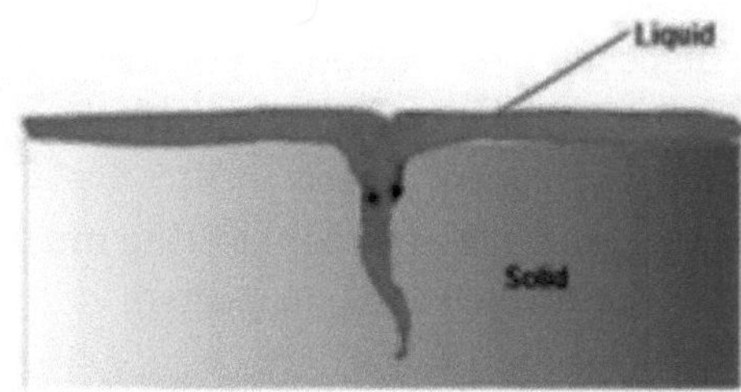

Fig 12. Penetrant Application

Penetrant Dwell:

The penetrant is left on the surface for a sufficient time to allow as much penetrant as possible to be drawn from or to seep into a defect. Penetrant dwell time is the total time that the penetrant is in contact with recommended by the penetrant producers or required by the specification being followed. The times vary depending on the application, penetrant materials used, the material, the form of the material being inspected, and the type of discontinuity being inspected for.Minimum dwell times typically range from five to 60 minutes. Generally, there is no harm in using a longer penetrant dwell time as long as the penetrant is not allowed to dry. The ideal dwell time is often determined by experimentation and may be very specific to a particular application.

Excess Penetrant Removal:

This is the most delicate part of the inspection procedure because the excess penetrant must be removed from the surface of the sample while removing as little penetrant as possible from defects.

Developer Application:

A thin layer of developer is then applied to the sample to draw penetrant trapped in flaws back to the surface where it will be visible. Developers come in a variety of forms that may be applied by dusting (dry powders). dipping, or spraying (wet developers).

Indication Development:

The developer is allowed to stand on the part surface for a period of time sufficient to permit the extraction of the trapped penetrant out of any surface flaws. This development time is usually a minimum of 10 minutes. Significantly longer times may be necessary for tight cracks.

Inspection:

Inspection is then performed under appropriate lighting to detect indications from any flaws which may be present.

Clean Surface:

The final step in the process is to thoroughly clean the part surface to remove the developer from the parts that were found to be acceptable.

Advantages

1. High sensitivity (small discontinuities can be detected).
2. Few material limitations (metallic and nonmetallic, magnetic and nonmagnetic, and conductive and nonconductive materials may be inspected). Rapid inspection of large areas and volumes.
3. Suitable for parts with complex shapes. Indications are produced directly on the surface of the part and constitute a visual representation of the flaw.
4. Portable (materials are available in aerosol spray cans)
5. Low cost (materials and associated equipment are relatively inexpensive)

Disadvantages

1. Only surface breaking defects can be detected.
2. Only materials with a relatively nonporous surface can be inspected.
3. Pre-cleaning is critical since contaminants can mask defects.
4. Metal smearing from machining, grinding. and grit or vapor blasting must be removed.
5. The inspector must have direct access to the surface being inspected.
6. Surface finish and roughness can affect inspection sensitivity.
7. Multiple process operations must be performed and controlled.
8. Post cleaning of acceptable parts or materials is required.
9. Chemical handling and proper disposal is required.

3.5 Magnetic Particle Inspection

- Magnetic particle inspection can detect both production discontinuities (seams, laps, grinding cracks and quenching cracks) and in-service damage (fatigue and overload cracks)
- Magnetism is the ability of matter to attract other matter to itself.
- Objects that possess the property of magnetism are said to be magnetic or magnetized and magnetic lines of force can be found in and around the objects.
- A magnetic pole is a point where the a magnetic line of force exits or enters a material.

Magnetic field lines:

- Form complete loops.
- Do not cross.
- Follow the path of least resistance.
- All have the same strength.
- Have a direction such that they cause poles to attract or repel.

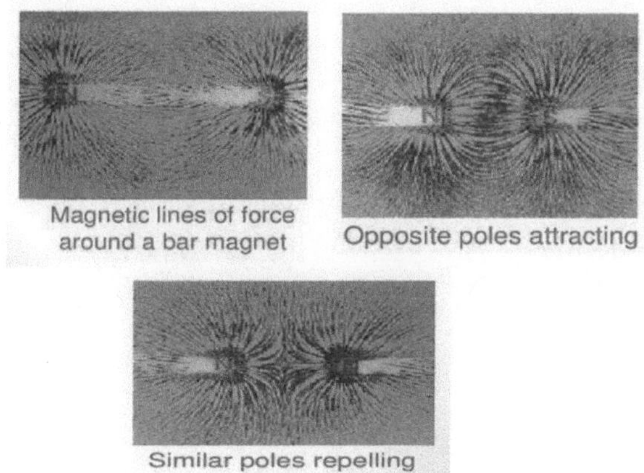

Fig 13. Magnetic field lines

How Does Magnetic Particle Inspection Work?

- A ferromagnetic test specimen is magnetized with a strong magnetic field created by a magnet or special equipment. If the specimen has a discontinuity, the discontinuity will interrupt the magnetic field flowing through the specimen and a leakage field will occur.

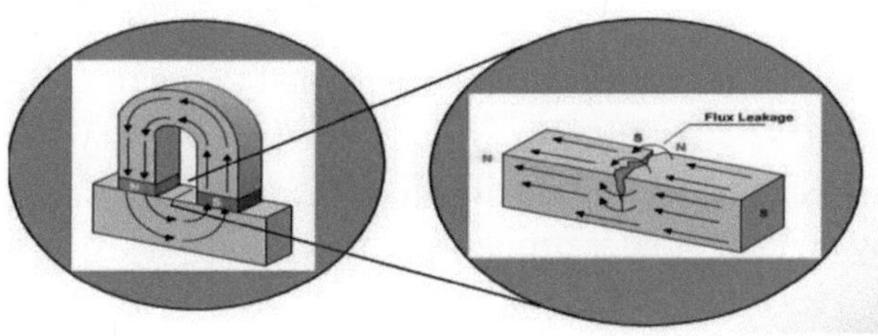

Fig 14. Magnetic Particle Inspection

Finely milled iron particles coated with a dye pigment are applied to the test specimen. These particles are attracted to leakage fields and will cluster to form an indication directly over the discontinuity. This indication can be visually detected under proper lighting conditions.

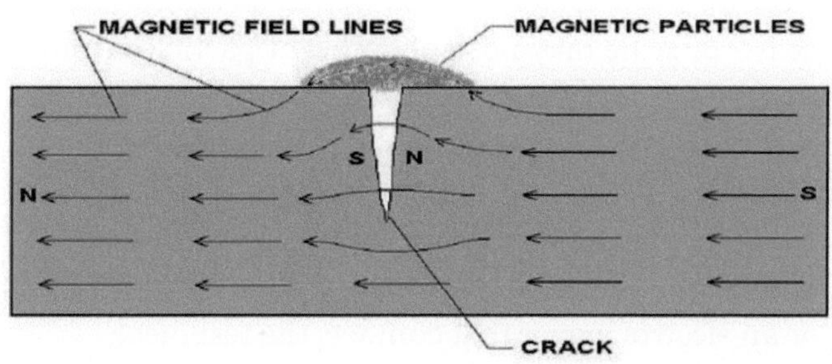

Fig 15. Magnetic Particle

Basics of Magnetic Particle Testing

- A ferromagnetic test specimen is magnetized with a strong magnetic field created by a magnet or Special equipment.
- If the specimen has a discontinuity, the discontinuity will interrupt the magnetic field flowing through the specimen and a leakage field will occur.

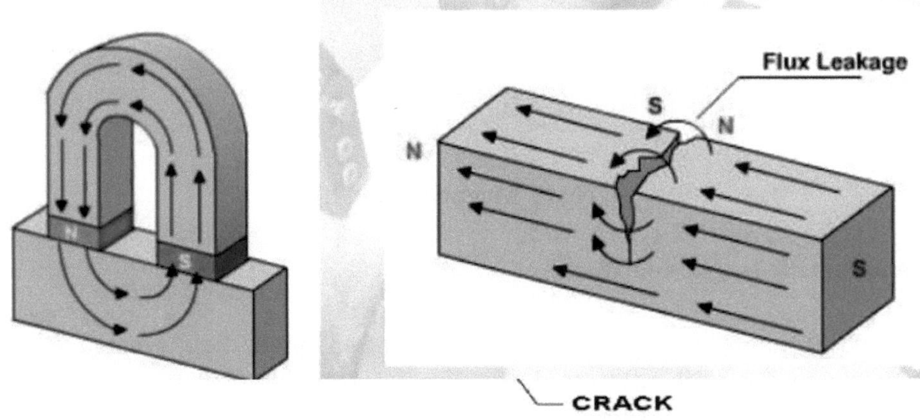

Fig 16. Magnetic Particle Testing

Finely milled iron particles coated with a dye pigment areapplied to the test specimen.

- These particles are attracted to leakage fields and will cluster to form an indication directly over the discontinuity.
- This indication can be visually detected under proper lightingconditions.

Basic steps involved:

- Component pre-cleaning
- Introduction of magnetic field
- Application of magnetic media
- Interpretation of magnetic particle indications

Pre-cleaning

- Contaminants such as oil, grease, or scale may not only prevent particles from being attracted to leakage fields, they may also interfere with Interpretation of indications.

Introduction of the Magnetic Field

- The required magnetic field can be introduced into acomponent in a number of different ways.
- Using a permanent magnet or an electromagnet that contacts the test piece
- Flowing an electrical current through the specimen.
- Flowing an electrical current through a coil of wire aroundthe part or through a central conductor running near the part.

Application of Magnetic Media (Wet Versus Dry)

- MPI can be performed using either dry particles, or particles suspended in a liquid.
- With the dry method, the particles are lightly dusted on to the surface. The dry method is more portable.
- With the wet method, the part is flooded with a Solution carrying the particles. The wet method is generally more sensitive since the liquid carrier gives the magnetic particles additional mobility.

Dry Magnetic Particles

- Magnetic particles come in a variety of colors.
- A color that produces a high level of contrast against the background should be used.

Fig 17. Dry Magnetic Particles

Wet Magnetic Particles

- Wet particles are typically supplied as visible or fluorescent.
- Visible particles are viewed under normal white light and fluorescent particles are viewed under black light.

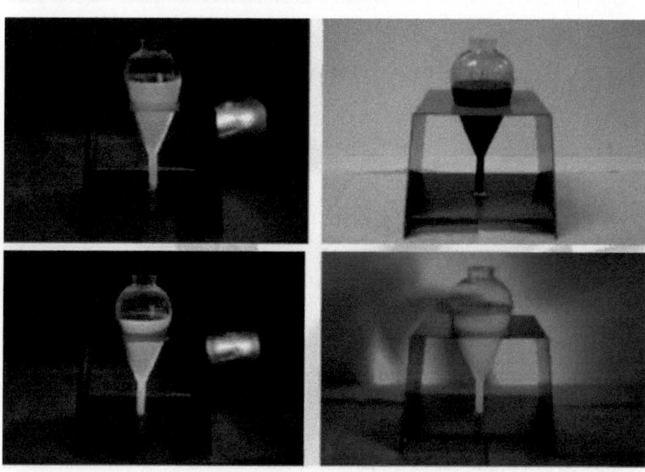

Fig 18. Wet Magnetic Particles

Interpretation of Indications

- After applying the magnetic field, indications that form must interpreted.
- This process requires that the inspector distinguish between relevant and non-relevant indications.

Fig 19. Crane Hook with Service Induced Crack

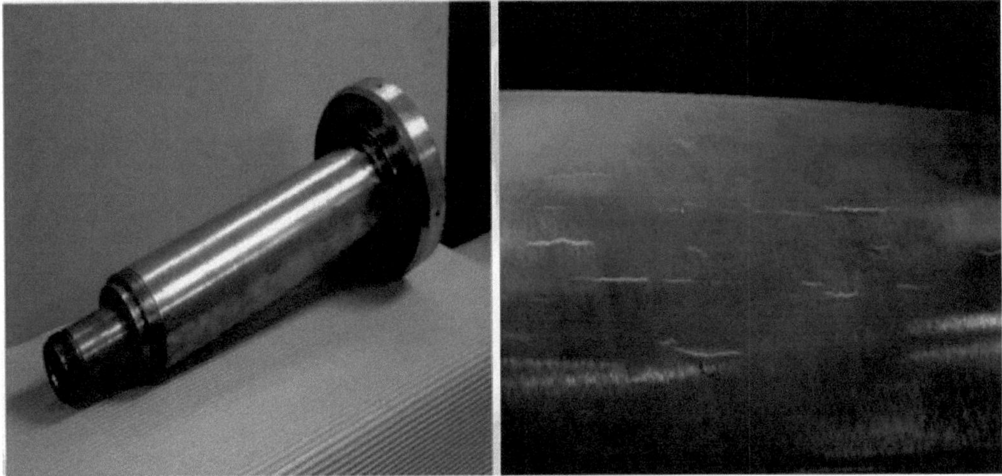

Fig 20. Drive Shaft with Heat Treatment Induced Cracks

Fig 21. Splined Shaft with Service Induced Cracks

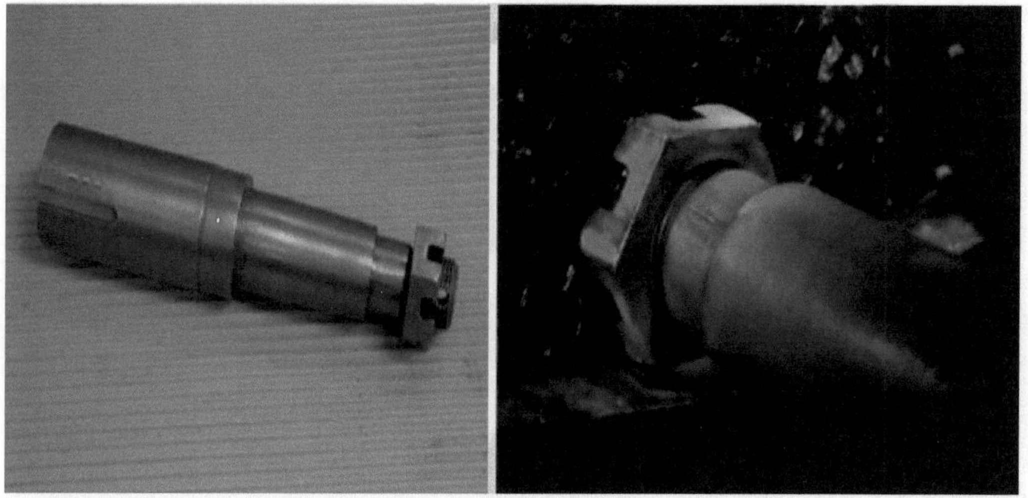

Fig 22. Threaded Shaft with Service Induced Crack

Fig 23. Threaded Shaft with Service Induced Crack

Fig 24. Crank Shaftt with Service Induced Crack Near Lube Hole

Demagnetization

- Parts inspected by the magnetic particle method may sometimes have an objectionable residual magnetic field that may interfere with subsequent manufacturing operations or service of the component.
- Possible reasons for demagnetization include:
- - May interfere with welding and/or machining operations
- -Can effect gauges that are sensitive to magnetic fields if placed in close proximity.
- -Abrasive particles may adhere to components surface and cause and increase in wear to engines components, gears, bearings etc.
- Demagnetization requires that the residual magnetic field is reversed and reduced by the inspector.
- This process will scramble the magnetic domains and reduce the strength of the residual field to an acceptable level.

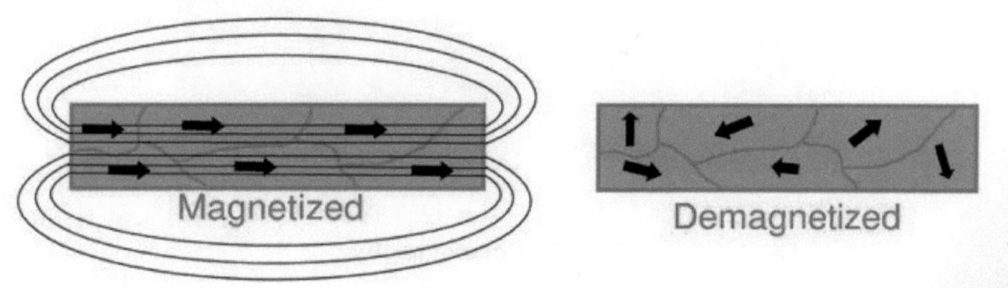

Fig 25. Demagnetization

Advantages of Magnetic Particle Inspection

- Can detect both surface and near sub-surface defects.
- Can inspect parts with irregular shapes easily.
- Precleaning of components is not as critical as it is for some other inspection methods. Most contaminants within a flaw will not hinder flaw detectability.
- Fast method of inspection and indications are visible directly on the specimen surface.
- Considered low cost compared to many other NDT methods.
- Is a very portable inspection method especially when used with battery powered equipment.

Limitations of Magnetic Particle Inspection

- Cannot inspect non-ferrous materials such as aluminum, magnesium or most stainless steels.
- Inspection of large parts may require use of equipment with special power requirements.
- Some parts may require removal of coating or plating to achieve desired inspection sensitivity.
- Limited subsurface discontinuity detection capabilities. Maximum depth sensitivity is approximately 0.6" (under ideal conditions).
- Post cleaning, and post demagnetization is often necessary.
- Alignment between magnetic flux and defect is important

3.6. Thermography Testing

- For decades, infrared (IR) pictures has been an acknowledged technique in military and security (imagers).
- Presently, IR Thermography has been becoming an important tool in nondestructive testing, technical diagnostics, as condition monitoring & predictive maintenance.
- Passive mode of Thermal NDT requires only using IR cameras.
- Active mode of Thermal NDT involves additional thermal stimulation of objects under test.
- Several types of heaters (coolers) are used in combination with IR cameras and computer stations.
- Recently, a new generation of IR imagers appeared, particularly suitable for different uses, sometimes specialized.
- Thermography's ability to see scenes, objects, and features otherwise invisible-sometimes even below a surface.
- It is used in a variety of applications for military, medical, industrial, agricultural, geological, meteorological, and energy conservational purposes.
- **What is thermography?**
- Infra Red Thermography is a technique for producing a visible image of invisible (to our eyes) infra red radiation emitted by objects due to their thermal conditions

Fig 26. Thermography

- IR thermography maps IR radiation flux (energy) and can determine heat flux and surface temperature
- It is Non-Destructive & Non-Contact
- It gives an image of the inspected object
- It works in real time
- Thermography is more and more extensively used for preventive maintenance, non-destructive testing and evaluation and quality control in the industry, buildings and medicine;
- Depending on the application of Thermographic NDT/E it may be applied alone or in conjunction with other metods Many objects need to be regularly inspected

Objectives of Test

- To detect hot or cold area's
- To determine absolute temperature
- To view Thermal profiles
- To detect temperature loss

Thermography

- Infra Red is part of the Electromagnetic Spectrum
- It travels in straight lines at the speed of light
- The useful part is divided between Short and Long wavelengths
- Use of the correct wavelength is essential

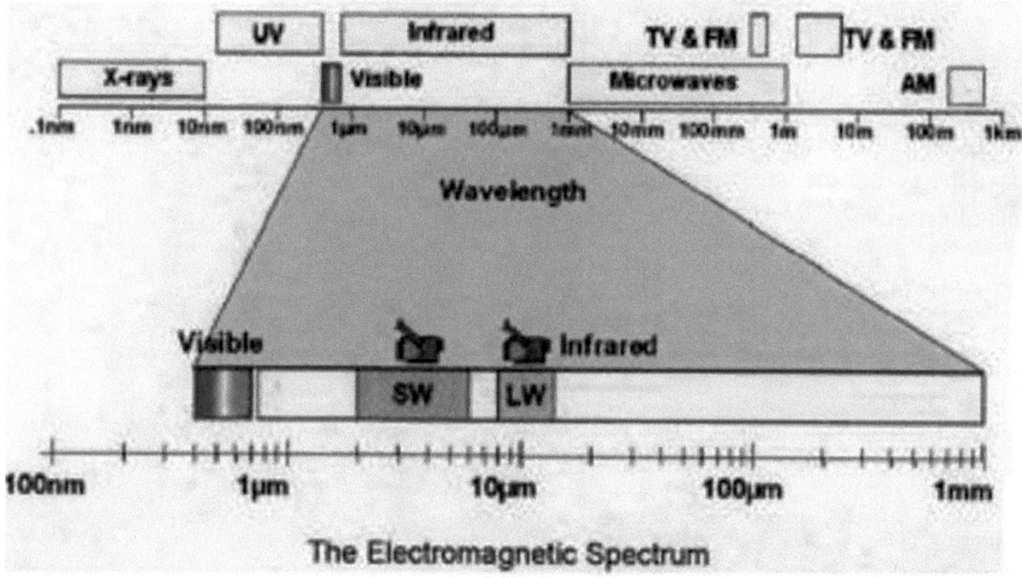

Fig 27. Infra Red

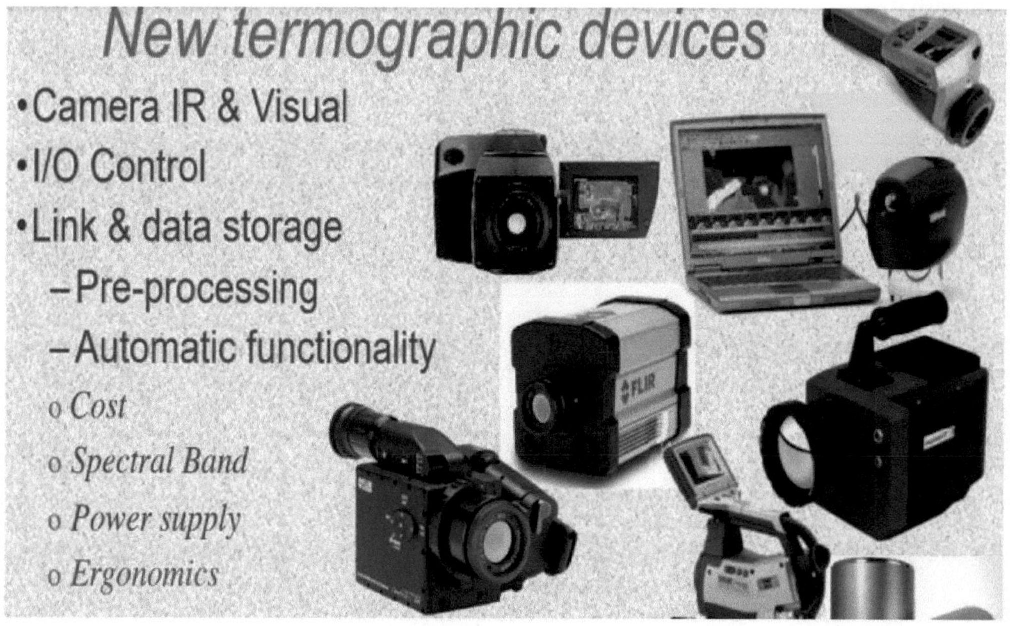

Fig 28. New Thermographic Devices

- Hand held portable camera
- Battery Powered Operating at correct wavelength
- Range.....-20°c to +1500°c
- Sensitivity.....0.1°c at 30°c
- Real time display
- Image Recording capability

- **Why Thermography?**

- Non Contact
- Rapid Scanning
- Data can be recorded in differing formats
- Images produced are comprehensive & reliable
- Is there a viable alternative?

Principles of Operation

- Object radiates infra red radiation.
- Temperature difference
- Differences are detected and displayed visually
- Emissivity values must be observed

Advantages

- Non Contact
- Non Intrusive
- Portable
- Can work at a distance
- Fast and Reliable
- Convincing Results

Limitations

- Non Intrinsically safe
- There must be a temperature difference for certain surveys
- Operator experience is essential
- Filters may be needed for certain applications
- Sensitivity and Resolution reduce with distance and angle of view

3.7 Electrical Testing

- Switch Gear
- Fuse boxes
- Cable runs
- Electrical connectors
- Insulation
- Transformers

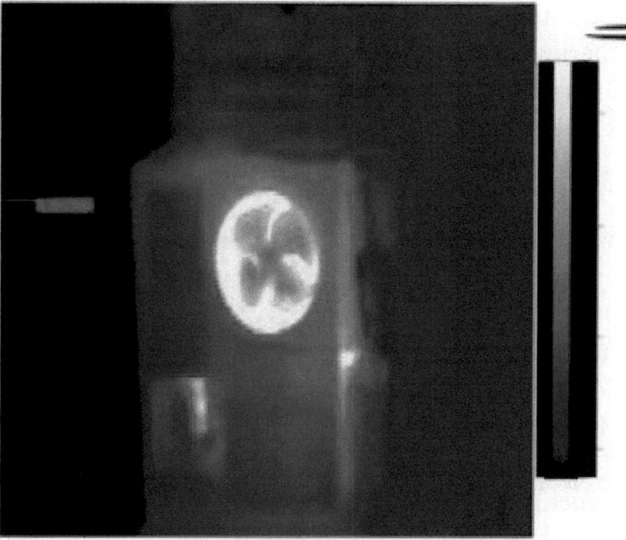

Fig 29. Fan

Fig 30. Junction Box

Electrical Connections

- Used for the detection of;
- Corroded connections
- Slack/loose connectors
- Connectors at too high an operating temperature
- Hot spots

Transformers

- Electrical connections
- Insulators
- Thermal profile
- Operating
- temperature
- Liquid Level

Building Surveys

- Used to detect:
- Lack of insulation
- Cold air infiltration Draughts
- Moisture traps
- Hot/warm air escaping
- Structural Integrity
- Heating/Cooling
- Moisture/Water Ingress
- Leaking Roof
- Bridged Cavity
- Leaking pipes

Process Plant

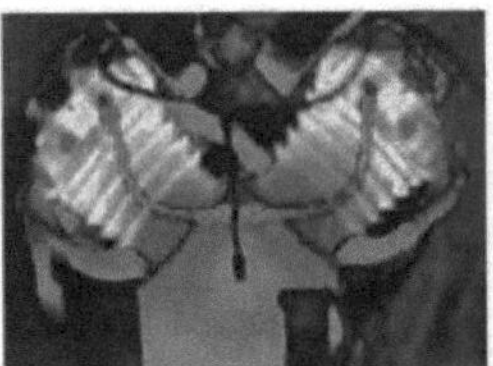

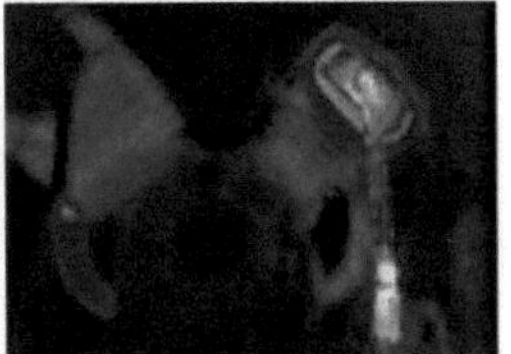

Fig 31.Process Plant

- The above Thermograms show how
- Thermography can be used as a very fast and effective maintenance tool.
- -The image on the right has a defective cylinder

Process Plant

- Thermography may be used for;
- Corrosion surveys
- Ensuring valve operation
- Leaks
- Blockages

3.8 Miscellaneous

- The detection of process or manufacturing faults
- Can be used as a quality control tool

3.8.1 Radiography Test

- Radiography is used in a very wide range of applications including medicine, engineering, forensics, security, etc.
- In NDT, radiography is one of the most important and widely used methods.
- Radiographic testing (RT) offers a number of advantages over other NDT methods,
- However, one of its major disadvantages is the health risk associated with the radiation.
- RT is one of the most widely used NDT methods for the detection of internal defects such as porosity and voids.
- With proper orientation of the X-ray beam, planar defects can also be detected with radiography.
- It is also suitable for detecting changes in material measurements and locating unwanted or defective components hidden from view in an assembled part.
- RT is method of inspecting materials for hidden flaws by using the ability of short wavelength electromagnetic radiation (high energy photons) to penetrate various materials.
- The intensity of the radiation that penetrates and passes through the material is either. captured by a radiation sensitive film (Film) Radiography) or by a planer array of radiation sensitive sensors (Real-time Radiography).
- Film radiography is the oldest approach, yet it is still the most widely used in NDT.

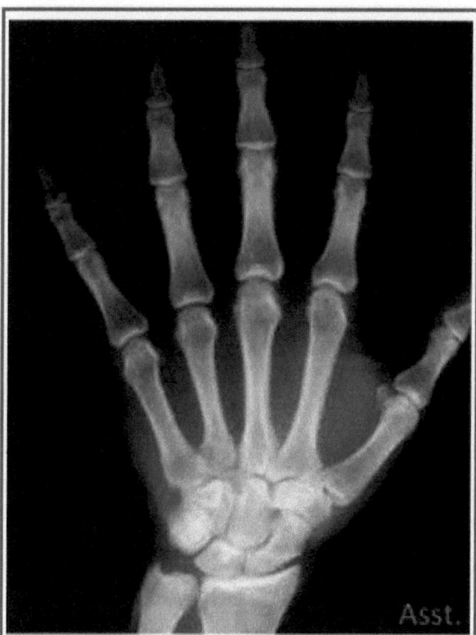

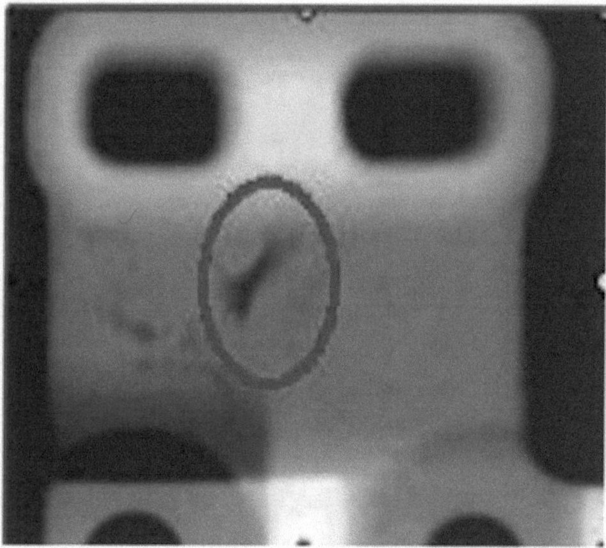

Fig 32. Radiography

Basic Principles

- In radiographic testing, the part to be inspected is placed between the radiation source and a piece of radiation sensitive film.
- The radiation source can either be an X-ray machine or a radioactive source.
- The part will stop some of the radiation where thicker and more dense areas will stop more of the radiation.
- The radiation that passes through the part will expose the film and forms a shadowgraph of the part.
- The film darkness (density) will vary with the amount of radiation reaching the film through the test object,
- where darker areas indicate more exposure (higher radiation intensity) and lighter areas indicate less
- The variation in the image darkness can be used to determine thickness or composition of material and would also reveal the presence of any flaws or discontinuities inside the material.

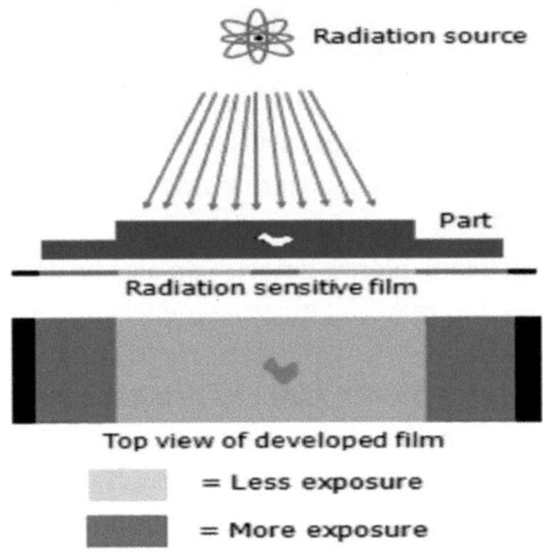

Fig 33. Radiation

- The energy of the radiation affects its penetrating power. Higher energy radiation can penetrate thicker and more dense materials.
- The radiation energy and/or exposure time must be controlled to properly image the region of interest.

Benefits of Radiographic Testing

- Can inspect assembled components
- Minimum surface preparation required
- Detects both surface and subsurface defects
- Provides a permanent record of the inspection
- Verify internal flaws on complex structures
- Isolate and inspect internal components
- Automatically detect and measure internal flaws Measure dimensions and angles within the sample without sectioning
- Sensitive to changes in thickness, corrosion, flaws and material density changes

Advantages of RT

- Both surface and internal discontinuities can be detected.
- Significant variations in composition can be detected.
- It can be used on a variety of materials.
- Can be used for inspecting hidden areas (direct access to surface is not required)
- Very minimal or no part preparation is required.
- Permanent test record is obtained.
- Good portability especially for gamma-ray sources.

Disadvantages

- Hazardous to operators and other nearby personnel.
- High degree of skill and experience is required for exposure and interpretation.

- The equipment is relatively expensive (especially for x-ray sources).
- The process is generally slow.
- Highly directional (sensitive to flaw orientation). • Depth of discontinuity is not indicated.
- It requires a two-sided access to the component.

Radiation Sources

- Two of the most commonly used sources of radiation in industrial radiography are x-ray generators and gamma ray sources. Industrial radiography is often subdivided into "X ray Radiography" or "Gamma Radiography", depending on the source of radiation used.

Fig 34. Radiation Sources

Nature of Penetrating Radiation

- Both X-rays and gamma rays are electromagnetic waves and on the electromagnetic spectrum they occupy frequency ranges that are higher than ultraviolet radiation.
- In terms of frequency, gamma rays generally have higher frequencies than X-rays. •
- The major distinction between X-rays and gamma rays is the origin where X-rays are usually artificially produced using an X-ray generator and gamma radiation is the product of radioactive materials.
- Both X-rays and gamma rays are waveforms, as are light rays, microwaves, and radio waves
- X-rays and gamma rays cannot be seen, felt, or heard. They possess no charge and no mass and, therefore, are not influenced by electrical and magnetic fields and will generally travel in straight lines.
- However, they can be diffracted (bent) in a manner similar to light.

Gamma Radiography

- Gamma rays are produced by a radioisotope.
- A radioisotope has an unstable nuclei that does not have enough binding energy to hold the nucleus together.
- The spontaneous breakdown of an atomic nucleus resulting in the release of energy and matter is known as radioactive decay.

X-ray Radiography

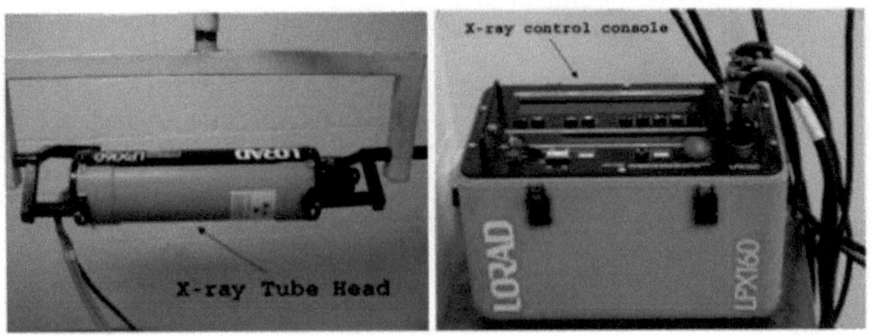

Fig 35. X-ray Radiography

Unlike gamma rays, x-rays are produced by an X-ray generator system. These systems typically include an X-ray tube head, a high voltage generator, and a control console.

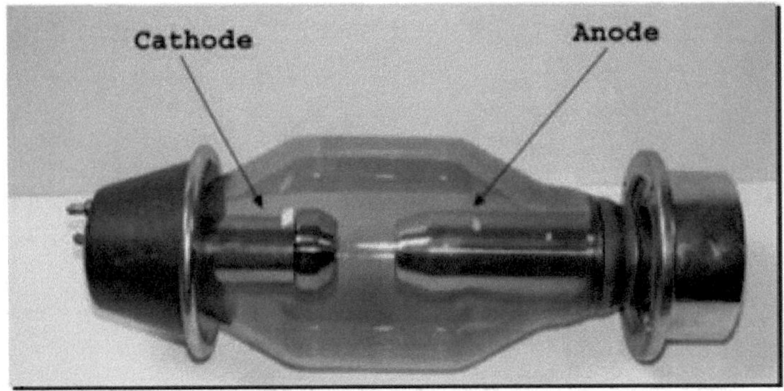

Fig 36. X-ray tube

- X-rays are produced by establishing a very high voltage between two electrodes, called the anode and cathode.
- To prevent arcing, the anode and cathode are located inside a vacuum tube, which is protected by a metal housing.

FOUR

MATERIAL CHARACTERIZATION TESTING

Principles, Types, Advantages and Limitations, Applications of

- Macroscopic and Microscopic observations
- Optical and Electron microscopy (SEM and TEM)
- Diffraction techniques
- Spectroscopic Techniques
- Electrical and Magnetic Techniques

4.1 Macroscopic and Microscopic observations
Why?:

1. Assess adequate/inadequate collection and transport
2. Orientation of diagnosis

4.1.1 Macroscopic examination
Assessment of collection & transport

- Integrity of package and sample container
- Quantity: adequate for required tests

4.1.2 Orientation of diagnosis
4.1.2.1 Cerebrospinal fluid (CSF)
- Normal aspect: clear liquid
- Pathologic aspects: colour, turbidity, deposits, clots
e.g:
fever, headache, neck stifness, photophobia + **turbid CSF**
-->(presumptive) bacterial meningitis
fever, headache, neck stifness, photophobia + **clear CSF**
-->(presumptive) viral meningitis
4.1.2.2 Pus
Colour - depends on presence of bacterial pigment
e.g.

1. Staphylococcus aureus - creamy, yellow pus

2. Pseudomonas aeruginosa - blue-greenish pus

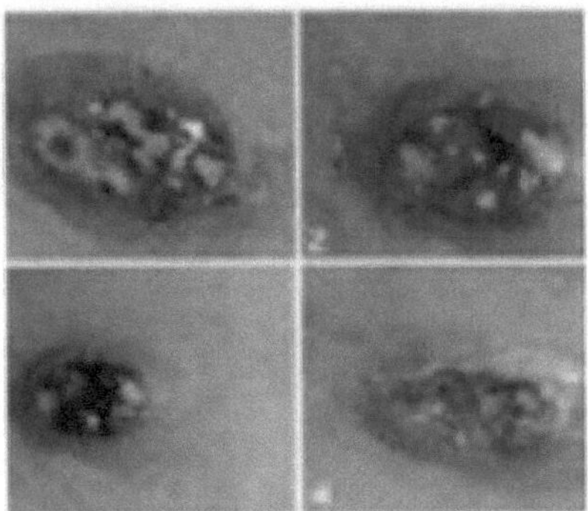

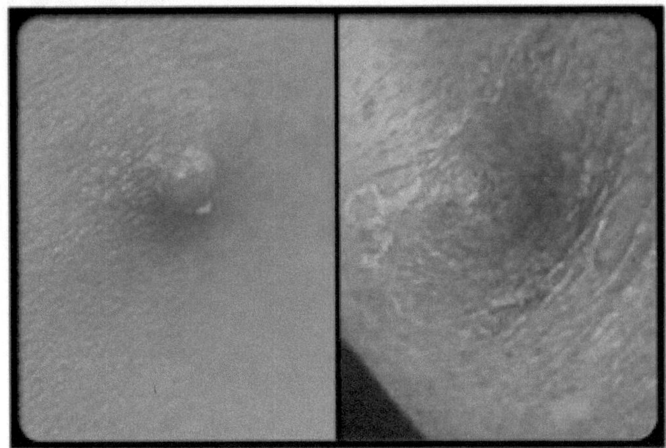

Fig 1 **Staphylococcus aures,creamy,yellow pus**

- Skin graft infected with Pseudomonas aeruginosa
- Pyocyanin - blue pigment produced by Ps. aeruginosa (pyocyanic bacillus)

4.2 Macroscopic Examination:
Orientation Of Diagnosis

Fig 2 **Urine**

4.3 Sputum

colour, consistency, adherence, presence of pus
e.g.

1. "rusty red pneumococcal pneumonia (presence of blood/blood pigments)
2. bright red tuberculosis (hemoptisys)
3. yellowish-white-presence of white blood cells (infection)

4.3.1 Type of sputum

- Bloody
- Rusty colored
- Purulent
- Foamy white
- Frothy pink

4.3.1.2 Faeces (stool)

- colour,
- consistency,
- presence of blood traces, mucus, pus - might indicate Salmonella, Shigella infections

4.4 Light(bright) Field Microscopy

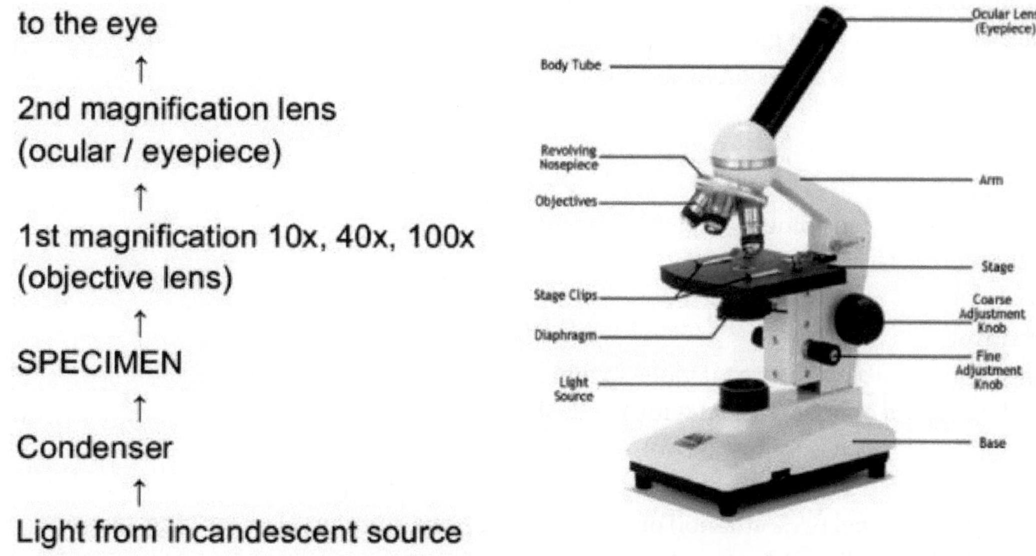

Fig 3 **Light(bright) Field Microscopy**

4.5 Objective lenses

- 10 x-general overview of sample

- 40 x - "large" microorganisms: fungi, parasites
- 100 x - bacteria
- **Wet mounts (unstained materials)**
- Direct light
- Observation of cells (PMN, macrophages), mobile germs in liquid samples (urine, CSF) shape and disposition of germs (cocci/bacilli/spirilli/vibrios)

Fig 4 **Wet mounts- Microscope glass slide and cover slip**

4.6 Stained smears

Smear specimen on microscope glass slide Dry (air)

Heat Fixation (flame): helps adhesion of specimen to slide, kills bacteria, favours absorbtion of stain on bacterial surface

Staining:

- Monostaining e.g. Methylene blue
- Combined (2 dyes) e.g. Gram, Ziehl Nielsen

4.7 Gram staining

1. heat-fixed smear flooded with crystal violet (primary stain)
2. crystal violet drained off and washed with distilled water
3. smear covered with "Gram's iodine" (Lugol) (mordant or helper)
4. iodine washed off: all bacteria appear dark violet or purple
5. slide washed with alcohol (95% ethanol) or an alcohol-acetone solution (decolorizing agent)
6. alcohol rinsed off with distilled water
7. slide stained with safranin, a basic red dye (counter stain)
8. smear washed again, heat dried and examined microscopically

Exact protocol - depending on the kit

4.8 Optical Microscopy

The optical microscopy, often referred to as light microscopy, is a type of microscopy which uses visible light and system of lenses to magnify images of small samples. Antonie van Leeuwenhook (1632-1674, studied on Spirogyra

-called animalcules, meaning "little animals") is credited with bringing the microscopy to the attention of biologists. There are two basic configuration of the conventional optical microscopy: the simple microscope and the compound microscope.

4.9 Simple Microscopy

A simple microscope is a microscope that uses a lens or set of lenses (single convex lens or groups of lenses) to enlarge an object through magnification alone, giving the viewer an erect enlarged virtual image. Simple microscopes are not capable of high magnification.

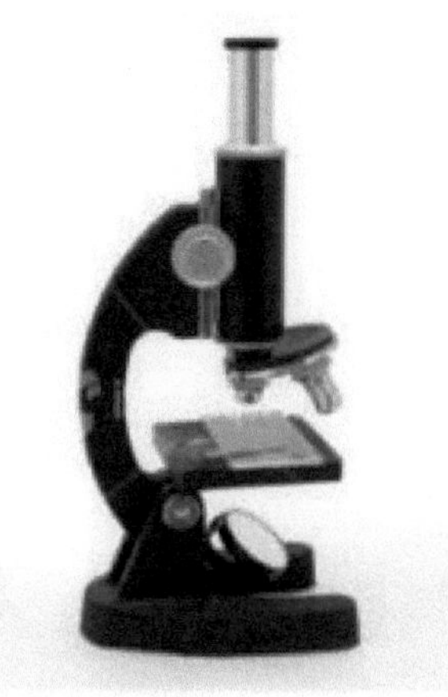

Fig 5 **Simple microscope**

4.10 Compound Microscope

A compound microscope is amicroscope which uses a lenses close to the object being viewed ti collect light (called the objective lenses)which focuses a real image of the object inside the microscope .The image is then magnified by a second lens or group of lenses (called the eyepiece) that gives the viewer an enlarged inverted virtual image of the object. The use of a compound objective/eyepiece combination allow for much higher magnification.

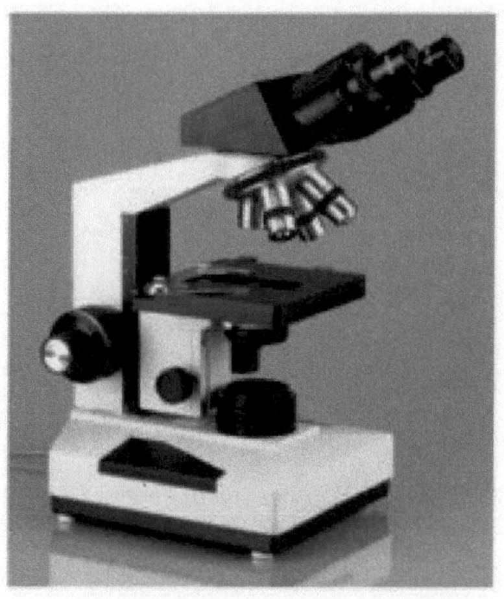

Fig 6 **Compound microscope**

4.10.1 Components:

1. stage (to hold the specimen)
2. Light sources(a light or a mirror)
3. Diaphragm and condenser
4. Mechanical stage

4.10.2 Advantages:

- Direct imaging with no need of sample pre treatment,the only microscopy for real color imaging.
- Fast,and adaptable to all kinds of sample systems,from gas,to liquid,and to solid sample systems,in any shapes or geometries.
- Easy to be integrated with digital camera systemfor data storage and analysis

4.10.3 Disadvantages:

Low resolution, usually down to only sub micron or a few hundreds of nanometers,mainly due to light diffraction limit.

4.10.4 Application:

1. Optical microscopy is used extensively in microelectronics nanophysics,biotechnology,pharmaceutics research, mineralogy, and microbiology.
2. Optical microscopy is used for medical diagnosis the field being termed histopathology when dealing with tissues, or in smear tests on free cells or tissue fragments.

4.11 Electron Microscopy

Von Borries and Ruska (1938) constructed the first Electron microscopy (EM). Objectives smaller than 0.2 micrometer (20 nanometer) such as virus and internal structure of cells can be examined by EM. In EM, a beam of electron is used instead of light.The resolution power of EM is far greater than that of other microscope due to the shorter wavelength of electron (100000 time shorter than light). Image produced by EM are black and white but they may be coloured artificially to accentuate certain detail. Instead of using the glass lenses,an EM is uses electomagnetic lenses to focus the beam of electrons on to a specimen.

4.11.1 CLASSIFICATION:

Four types of EM Transmission electron microscopy (TEM)

1. Scanning electron microscopy (SEM)
2. Reflection electron microscopy
3. Scanning transmission electron microscopy

4.12 Transmission Electron Microscopy(TEM)

- 1000 time better resolutions that light microscope.
- Magnification is 10,000X-100,000X
- Can resolve the objects as closer to as 2.5 nm

4.12.1 Principle:

- **In TEM, a beam of electrons from an electron gun pass through the ultrathin specimen by electromagnetic condenser lens.**

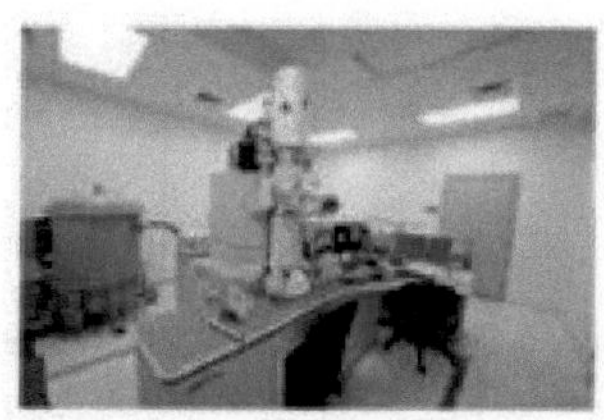

Fig 7 **Transmission electron microscopy**

After this the beam passes through the electromagnetic objective lens which magnify the image. Finally,the electrons are focused by an electromagnetic projector lens on to a fluorescent or photograaphic plate. The image appears many light and dark areas depending upon the number of electrons absorb by the different are of the sample .The image is known as TEM.

4.12.2 Sample preparation:

The sample must be 100 nm thick and able to maintain the integrity of the structure when bombarded with electrons beam under high vacuum. So it is necessary to support the sample by plastic. Fixation of specimen: is done by the chemicals like Glutaraldehyde or osmium tetraoxide to stabilize the structure. Dehydration of sample by acetone or ethanol. The sample is treated with un-polymerized, liquid epoxy plastic until the completely permeated and harden to form the solid block. The block cut into ultrafine size by microtome (100 nm) or diamond knife. Because the sample is very thing, the contrast between the structure and background is poor which can be increase by positive staining (specimen stain) of negative staining (background stain) to enhance the contrast.

4.12.3 Limtation:

- Poor penetration power of electron resulting a very thing sample is required (100 nm).
- Give only 2D image.
- Sample must be dehydrated, fixed and viewed under the high vacuum. This treatment not only kill the specimen but cause some shrinkage and distortion.
- Additional structure may observe know as artifets.

4.13 Scanning Electron Microscopy(SEM)

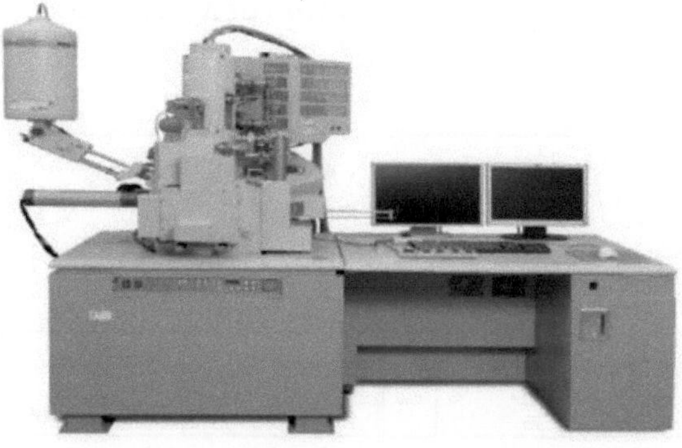

Fig 8 **Scanning electron microscopy**

In SEM, an electron beam produces a beam of electron called as primary beam. The electron passes through electromagnetic lenses and directed over the surface of specimen. >The primary electron beam knocks the surface of specimen resulting the generation of secondary electron beam that transmitted to an electron collector, amplified and used to produce an image on the screen or photographic plate. Magnification is 10,00X-10,000X

4.13.1 Resolution:

Resolution is the minimum distance apart that 2 objects can be in order for them to appear as separate items. The greater resolutions the clearer the image.

$d = 1.22\ \lambda/NA$

Where d is the resolving power, A is the wavelength, NA is the numerical aperture.

$NA = n \sin u$

n= the lowest refractive index between the object and first objective element u=is the 1/2 the angular aperture of the objective

4.13.2 Advantages:

- Almost all kinds of samples, conducting and non conducting (stain coating needed).
- SEM overcomes the problems associated with TEM.
- It gives the 3D structure.

4.13.3 Disadvantages:

- Low resolutions, usually above a few tens of nanometers.
- Usually required surface stain-coating with metals for electron conducting.

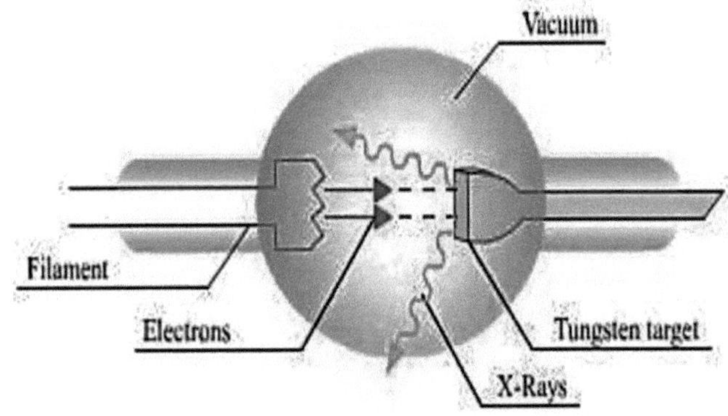

Fig 9 **Generation of X-RAYS**

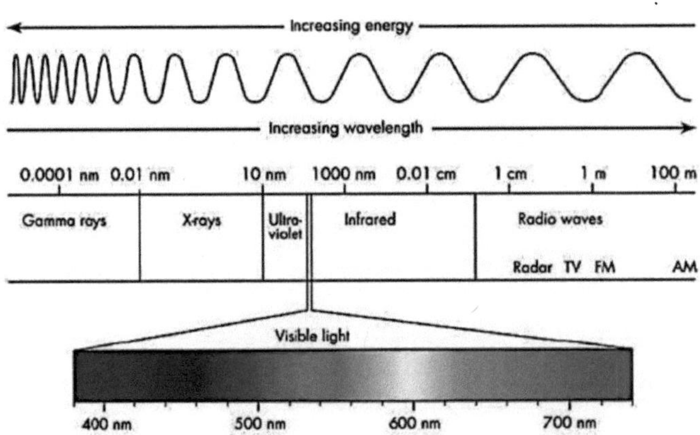

Fig 10 **X-RAY Region**

4.14 X-RAY Diffraction (XRD)

- These methods are based on the scattering of X-ray crystals.
- When x-rays interact with a solid material, the scattered beams causes diffraction.

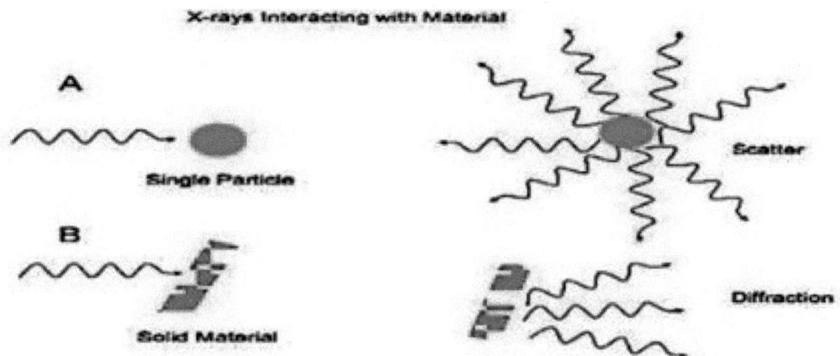

Fig. 11 **X-RAY Diffraction**

4.15 XRD Principle

Different Planes in a crystal give different signa equal to positive interface of waves.

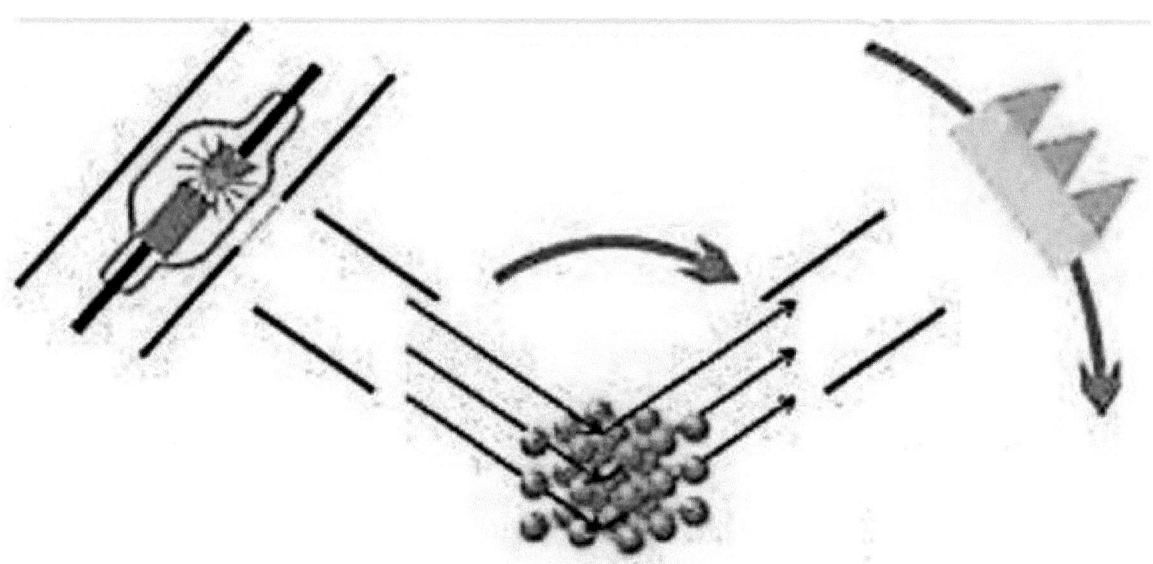

Fig 12 **XRD Principle**

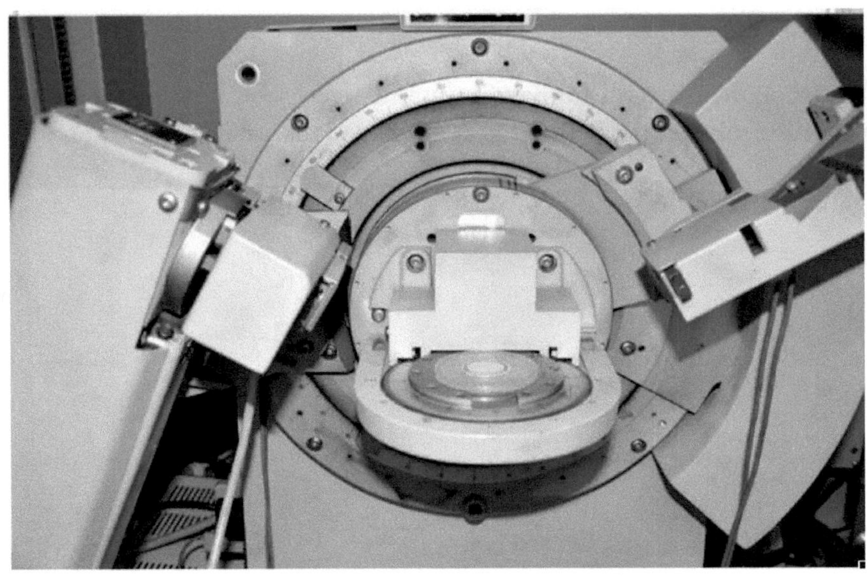

Fig 13 **XRD Equipment**

4.15.1 Experimental Diffraction Methods

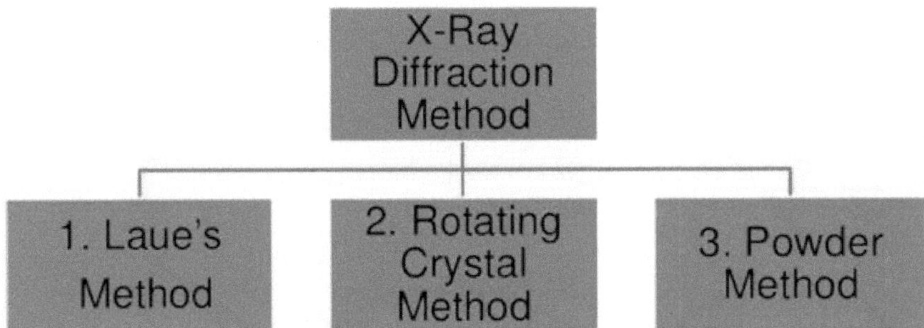

Fig 14 **Experimental Diffraction Methods**

4.16 Laue's Method

In this method a single crystal is held stationary in the path of radiation of continuous wavelength. While is kept constant, the wavelength, is varied. A plane film receives the diffracted beams. A developed film after its exposure shows a diffraction pattern that consists of series of spots.

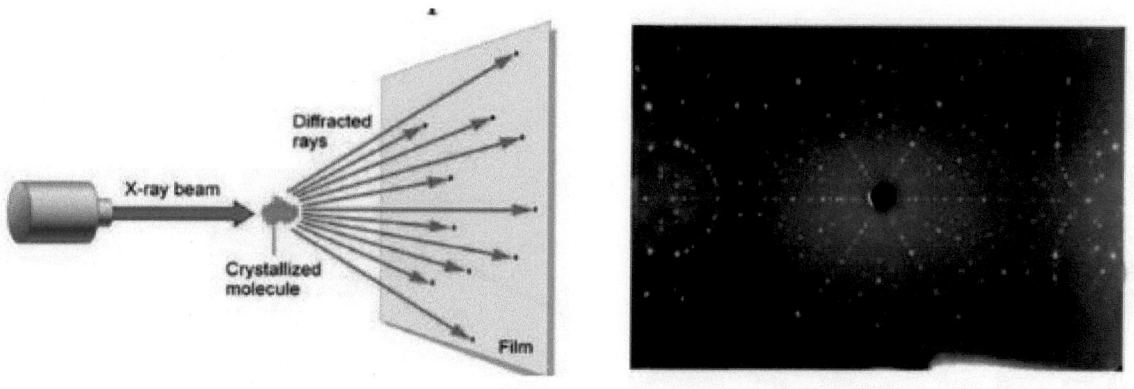

Fig 15 **Laue's Method**

4.16.1 Laue's method is divided into two types

- Transmission Method
- Back Reflection Method

4.16.2 A)Transmission Method

A beam of x-ray is passed through the crys after passing through the crystal, x-rays are diffrac and recorded on a photographic plate.

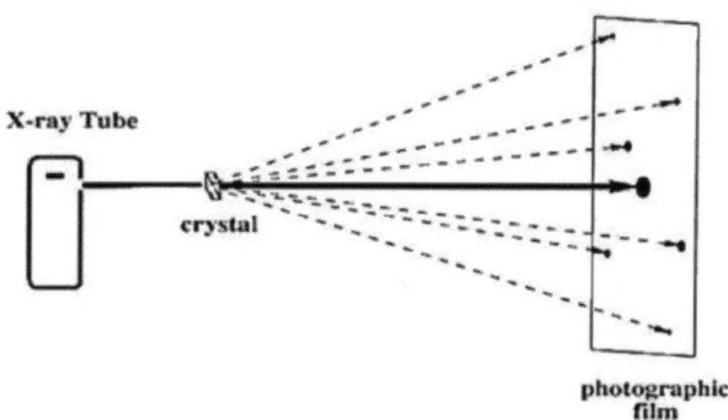

Fig 16 a **Transmission Method**

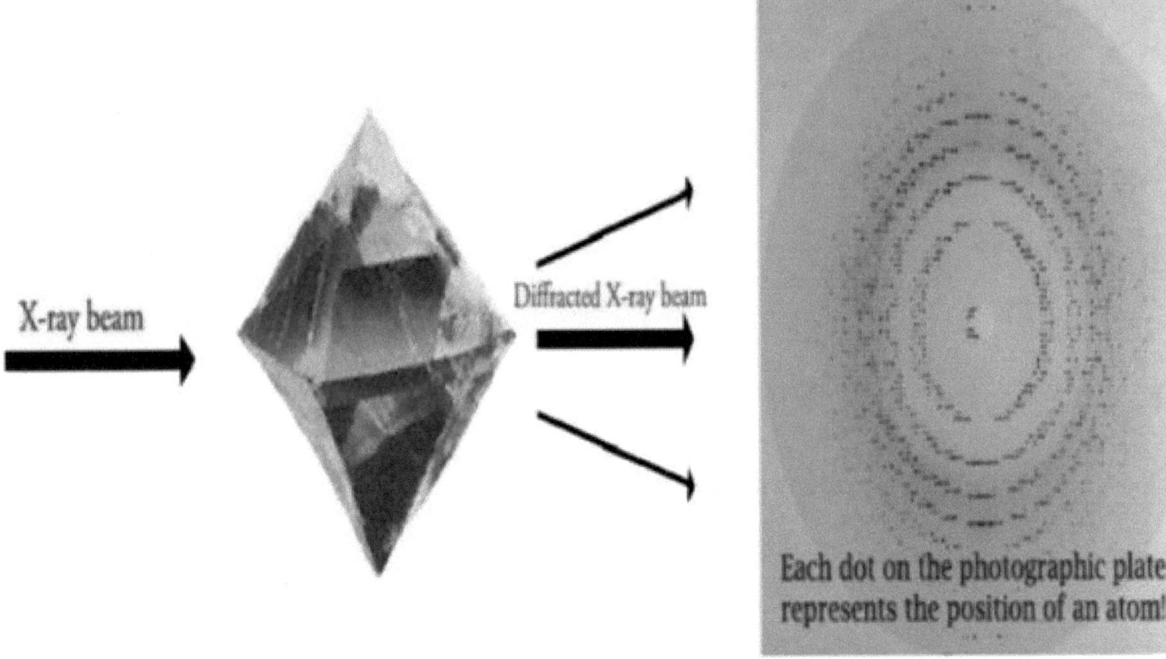

Fig 16 b **Transmission Method**

4.16.3 B)Back Reflection Method

This method provides similar information as the transmission method.

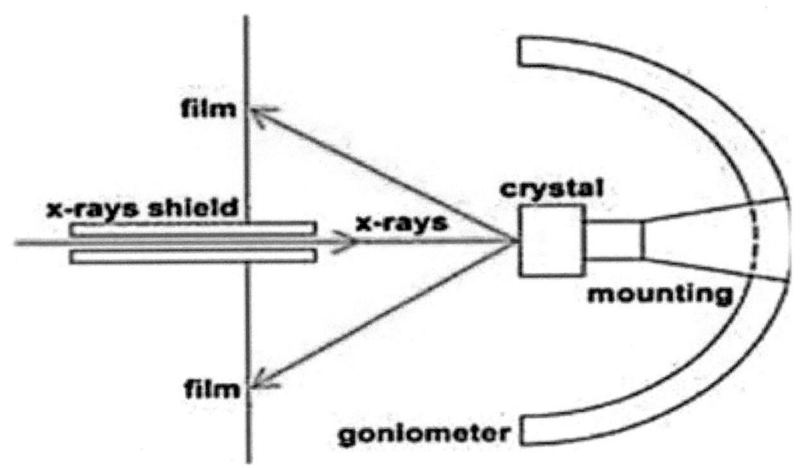

Fig 17 **Back Reflection Method**

4.17 ROTATING CRYSTAL METHOD

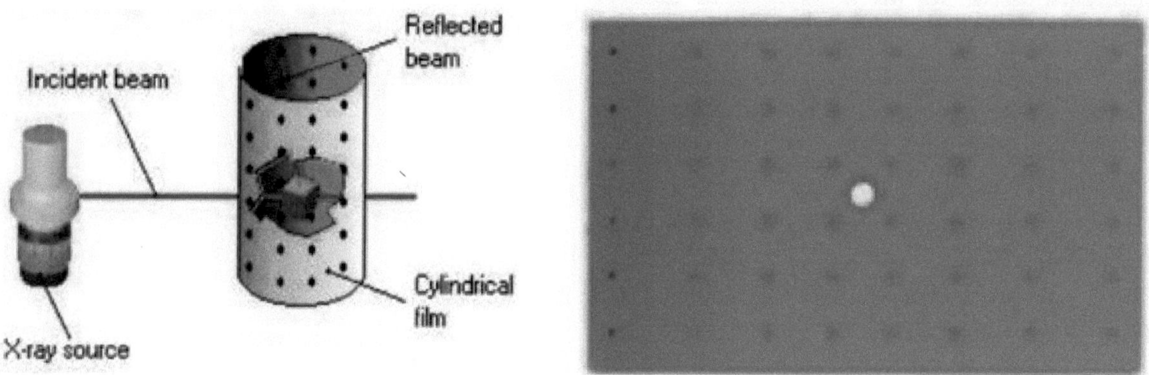

Fig 18 **ROTATING CRYSTAL METHOD**

- In this method, a single crystal is rotated about the fixe axis in a beam of monochromatic. The angle is variabl while the wavelength is kept constant.
- The variation of angle e due to rotation of the crystal bring different atomic planes in the crystal into position.
- To record such reflections a film is mounted on a cylindrica holder that is concentric with a rotating spindle.

4.18 Powder Method

- This method is useful for samples that are difficult to obtain in single crystal form.
- The powder method is used to determine the value of the lattice parameters accurately.

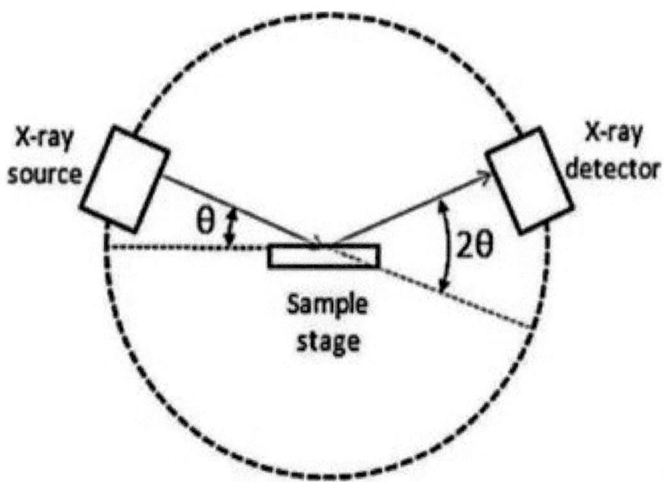

Fig 19 **Powder Method**

- A sample of hundreds of powdered crystals show that the diffracted beams form continuous cones.
- A circle of film is used to record the diffraction pattern.

- Each cone intersects the film giving diffraction lines.
- The lines are seen as arcs on the film.

4.19 Applications Of XRD Methods

- Determination of crystal size and shape.
- Particle size determination by spot counting methods.
- Crystallographic structural analysis.
- Unit cell calculations for crystalline materials.
- Identification of single and multi phase materials

4.20 Electrical Characterization Techniques

4.20.1 Electrical Parameters:

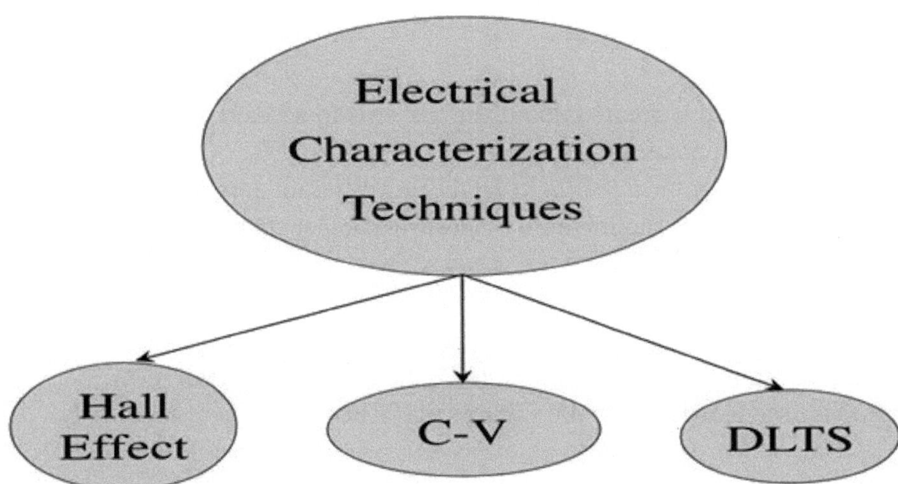

Fig 20 **Electrical Parameters**

- Carrier concentration (ionized donors, acceptors)
- -Carrier type (electrons or holes)
- Carrier mobility

4.20.2 Hall Effect

- The Hall effect is the deflection of electrons (holes) in an n-type (p-type) semiconductor with current flowing perpendicular to a magnetic field.
- The deflection of these charged carriers sets up a voltage, called the Hall voltage, whose polarity depends on the effective charge of the carrier.

4.20.3 Theory

- When a conductive plate is connected to a circuit with a battery, then a current starts flowing.
- The charge carriers will follow a linear path from one end of the plate to the other end.

- The motion of charge carriers results in the production of magnetic fields.
- When a magnet is placed near the plate, the magnetic field of the charge carriers is distorted.
- This upsets the straight flow of the charge carriers.
- The force which upsets the direction of flow of charge carriers is known as Lorentz force.

4.20.4 Applications of Hall Effect

- Hall effect principle is employed in the following cases:
- Magnetic field sensing equipment
- For the measurement of direct current, Hall effect Tong Tester is used.
- It is used in phase angle measurement
- Proximity detectors
- Hall effect Sensors and Probes
- Linear or Angular displacement transducers
- For detecting wheel speed and accordingly assist the anti-lock braking system.

4.21 Magnetometer

- Smart phones are equipped with magnetic compass.
- These compass measure Earth's magnetic field using 3-axis magnetometer.
- These magnetometer are sensors based on Hall Effect.
- These sensors produce a voltage proportional to the applied magnetic field and also sense polarity.

4.22 Current sensor

- A current sensor is a device that detects and converts current to an easily measurable output voltage, which is proportional to the current through the measured path.
- There are a wide variety of sensors, and each sensor is suitable for a specific current range and environmental condition.

4.22.1 Advantages

- Without magnetic core, it can lower the height. The internal structure can be much simpler so that it can reduce the cost.
- There is no hysteresis.
- Current consumption is low.
- 4. Temperature-Dependent hall effect/conductivity
- Can determine scattering mechanisms by using temperature-dependent measurements

1. At low T, ionized impurity scattering dominates
2. At high T, phonon scattering dominates

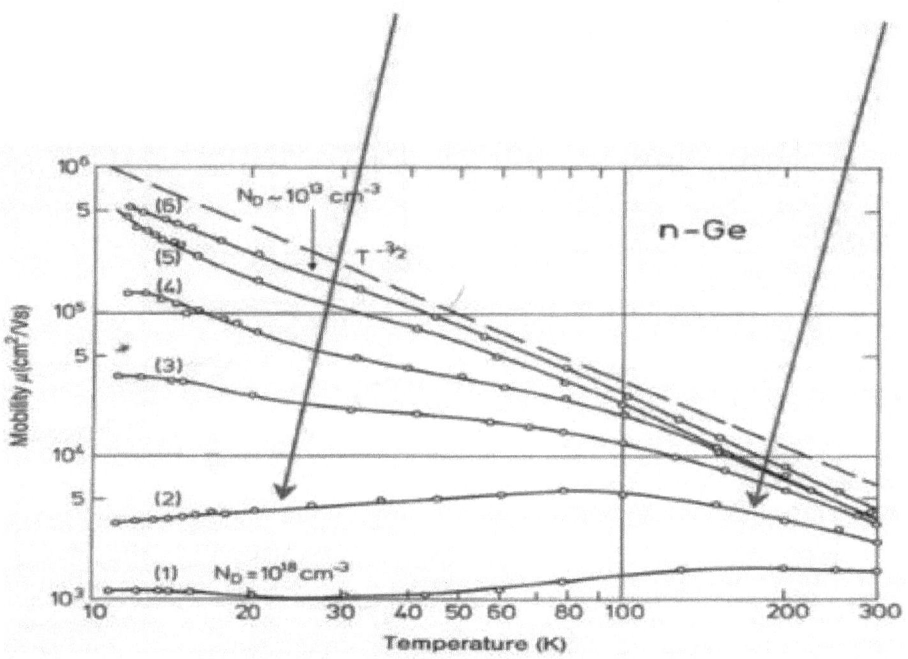

Fig 21 a **Hall Effect**

Can determine scattering mechanisms by using temperature-dependent measurements

1. At low T, ionized impurity scattering dominates
2. At high T, phonon scattering dominates

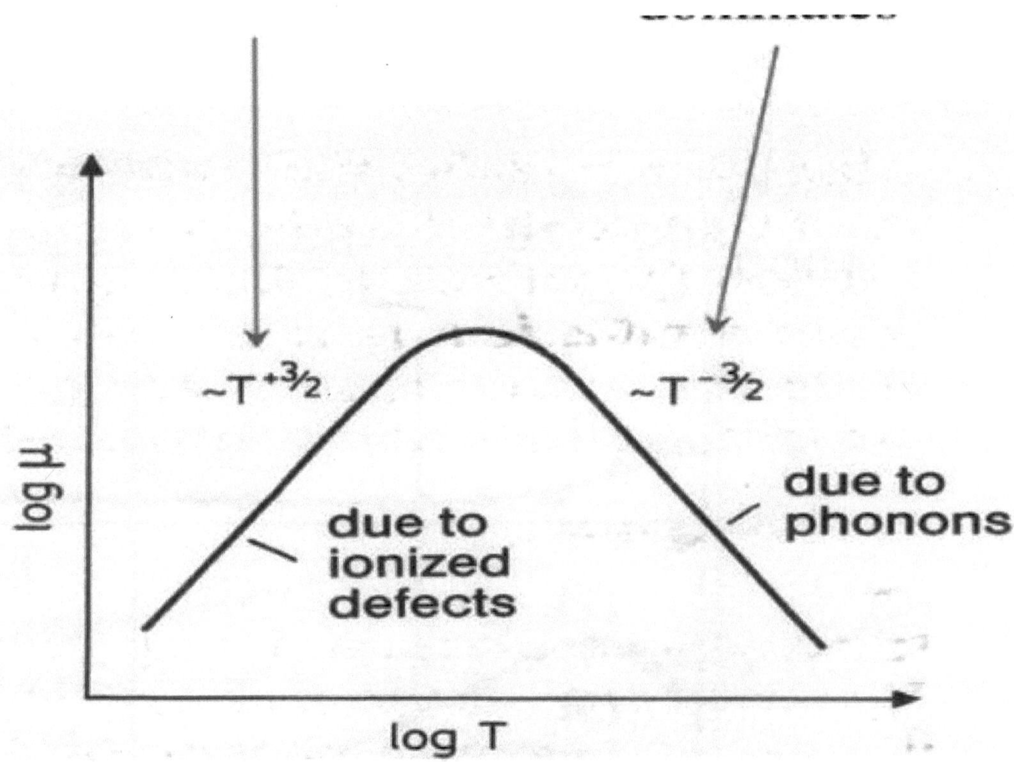

Fig 21 b **Hall Effect**

4.23 Temperature-Dependent Hall Effect

- Can determine donor or acceptor energy levels

n-exp [-(Ec- ED)/kT]

- Donors become increasingly ionized as T increases
- slope of Arrhenius plot (log n vs 1/T) → Ec-Ed
- Apply small ac signal (dV- 10 mV @ 1 MHz) on top of dc reverse bias
- Depletion width varies (dW) with ac signal (dV)
- Causes donor ionization over width dw
- Measure capacitance change
- Can determine n = ND*

$$C = \varepsilon A/W$$
$$dQ = -e N_D^+ A\, dW$$
$$C = -dQ/dV = eA N_D^+ dW/dV$$
$$N_D^+ = \frac{2}{e\varepsilon A^2 [\, d(1/C^2)/dV \,]}$$

- Can determine N_D^+ from slope of $1/C^2$ versus V

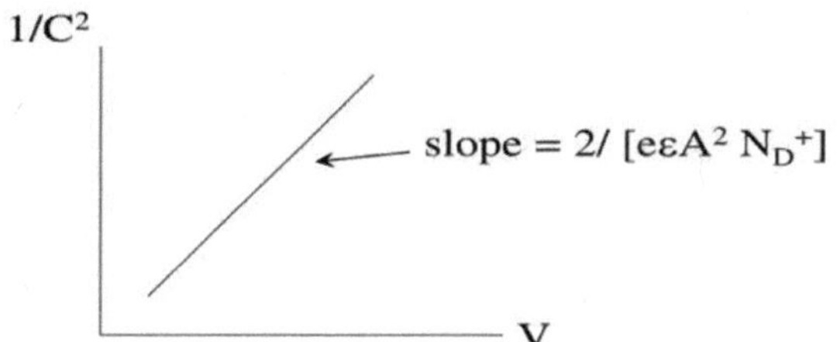

- Can convert voltage scale to depth scale by $W = \varepsilon A/C$

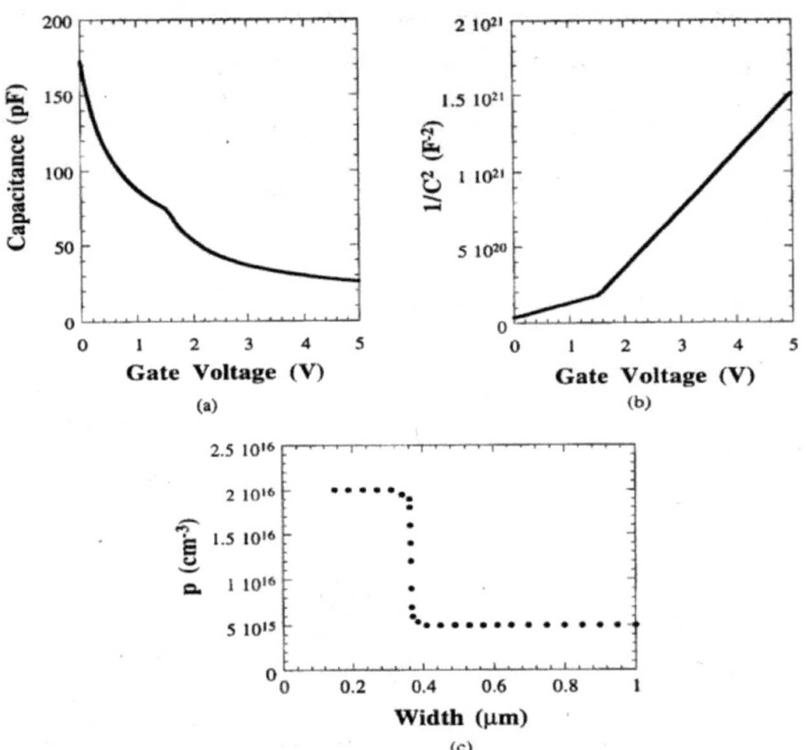

Usually assume n = ND = ND*:

- All donors become ionized
- Minority carriers are neglected
- All majority carriers in depletion region are removed

4.23.2 Disadvantage:

Maximum depth is limited by electrical breakdown at high reverse bias

4.24 C-V Profiling:

Can perform C-V measurement while performing a chemical etch

4.25 Electrochemical C-V Profiling

- Replace metal contact with electrolytic solution
- Destructive method

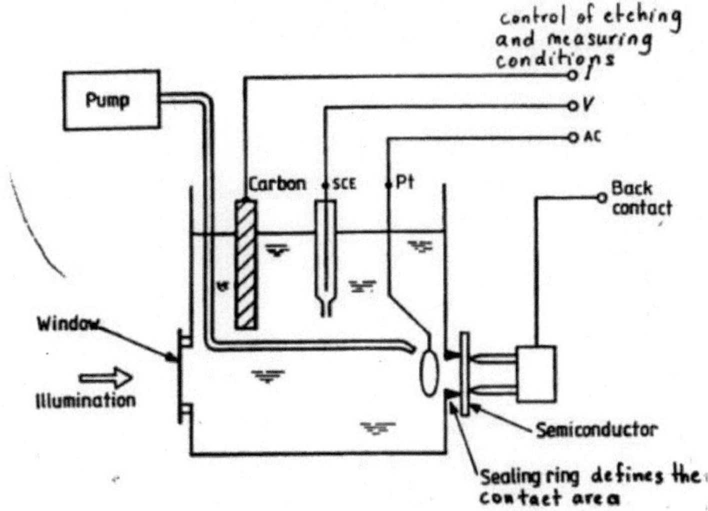

Fig 22 **Electrochemical C-V Profiling**

4.25.1 DLTS

• Deep level transient spectroscopy

• What are traps?

• Unwanted impurities or crystal defects

→e.g., Fe, Au in InP, GaAs Introduces discrete energy levels in the bandgap, usually near midgap Trap electrons or holes

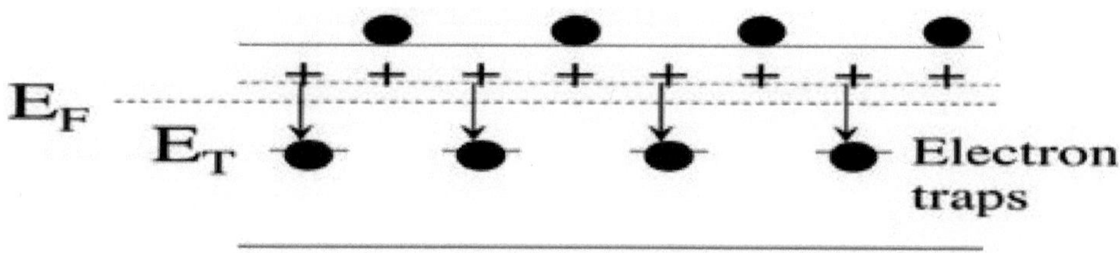

Fig 23 **DLTS**

4.25.2 Electron traps

- Negative when an e- is captured
- Neutral when empty
- Acceptor-like

4.25.3 Hole traps

- Positive when a hole is captured
- Neutral when empty

- Donor-like
- Requires Schottky diode or p-n junction
- e.g., apply metal contacts to sample to form Schottky diode
- Apply reverse bias pulse and measure capacitance transient
- Gives:

1. NT vs W
2. NT energy levels

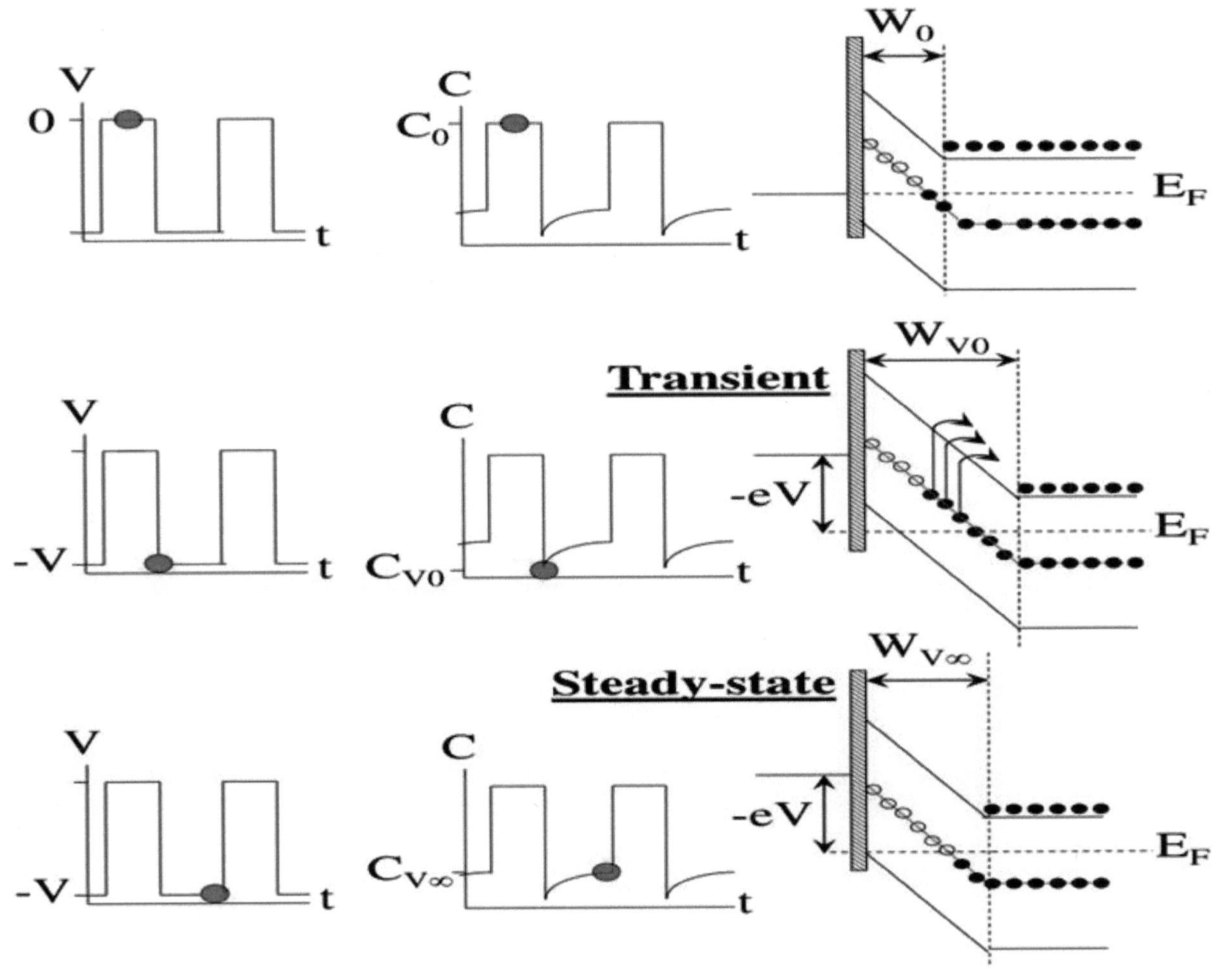

Fig 24 **NT vs W**

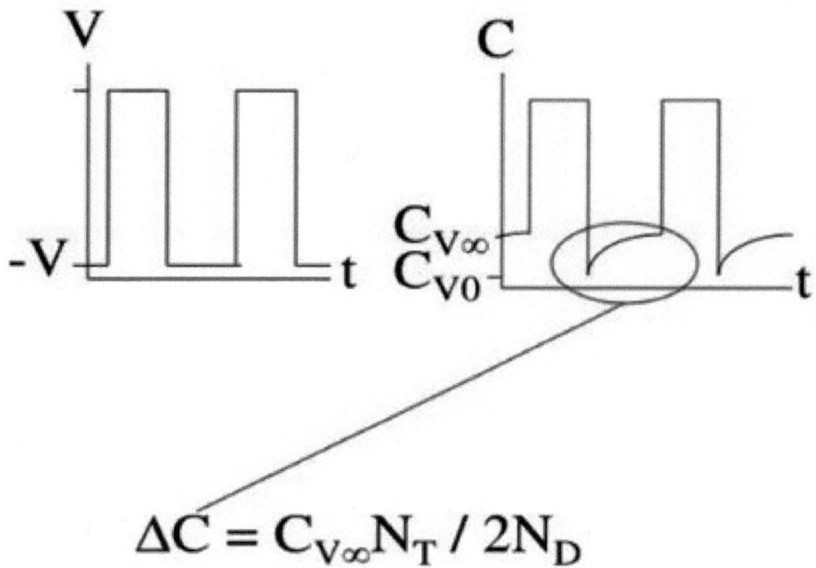

Fig 25 **NT energy levels**

Capacitance transient is characteristic of the emission of electrons from the traps:
AC(t)= AC exp (-e,t) emission rate
e-exp[-(E. - ET)/kT]
AC(t) = AC exp (e,t) e-exp[-(E, – Ep)/kT]
Capacitance transient varies with temperature

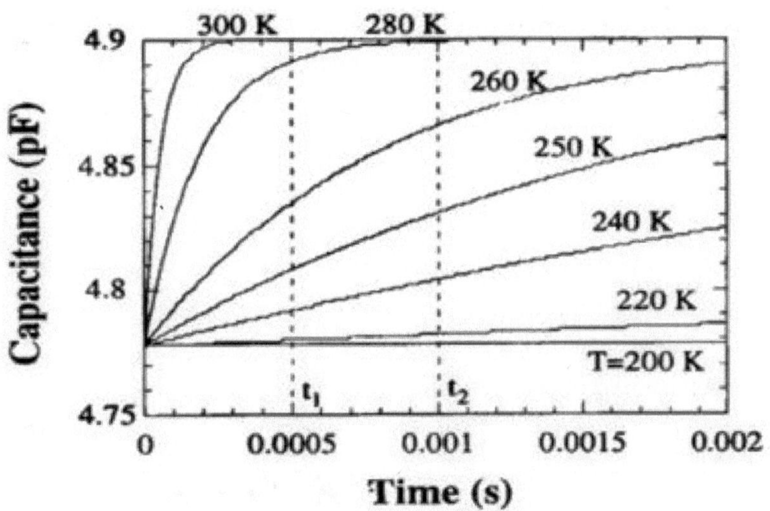

Fig. 26. Capacitance Vs Time

4.26 Spectroscopy Technique

- Spectroscopic techniques are used to study the interaction at the molecular scale.
- One such technique is nuclear magnetic resonance (NMR).
- To study the interaction between mucus and polymer proton and/or carbon NMR is used or NMR diffusion measurement can also elaborate such an interaction.

4.26.1 Spectroscopy

- ·Exactly how light is absorbed and reflected, transmitted, or refracted changes the info and is determined by different techniques

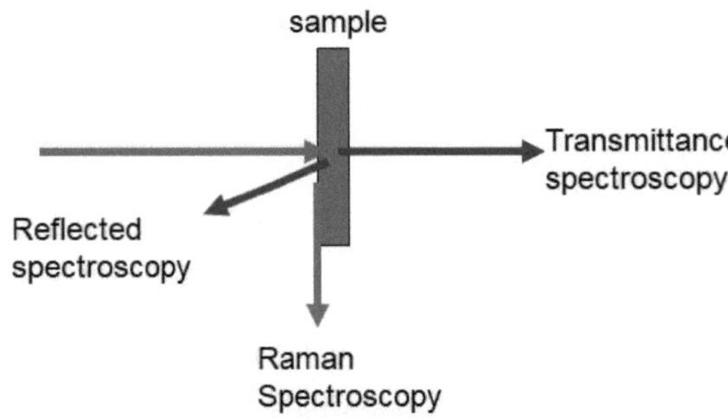

Fig 27 **Spectroscopy**

4.27 Optical Spectroscopy

- Techniques concerned with how light reflects, absorbs, or transmits through minerals from near UV to mid-infrared (250 – 3000 nm wavelengths)
- Dealing with energy which excited electrons from a standard to an excited state
- It uses light source for analysis.

4.27.1 USES

- Gives information about electronic structure of a system.
- Key technique in semiconductor research.
- To study the interaction of matter and light.
- Widely used in industry and quality assurance.

4.28 Reflectance Spectroscopy

- Can be optical or vibrational.
- Non-destructive form of analysis, used to 'see' some of the chemistry, bonding.
- Spectroscopy is particularly good at detecting water and OH groups in minerals (especially in IR).
- Good at differentiating between different clays because it detects OH groups well.

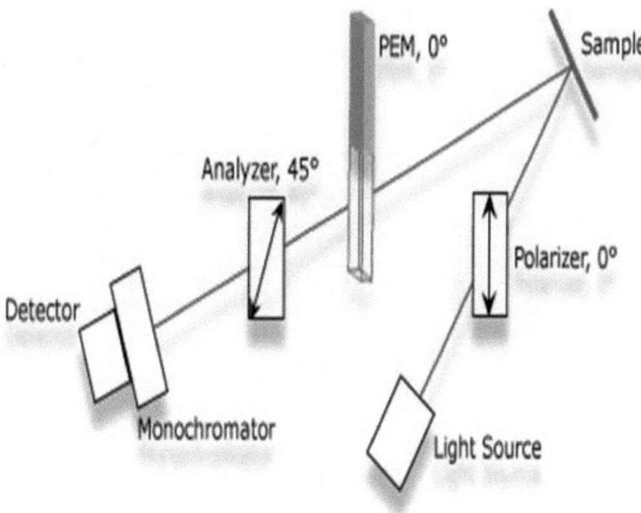

Fig 28 **Reflectance Spectroscopy**

4.29 Raman Spectroscopy

- ·Another kind of spectroscopy which looks at a scattering effect and what that tells us about the chemistry, oxidation state, and relative proportions of different ions.

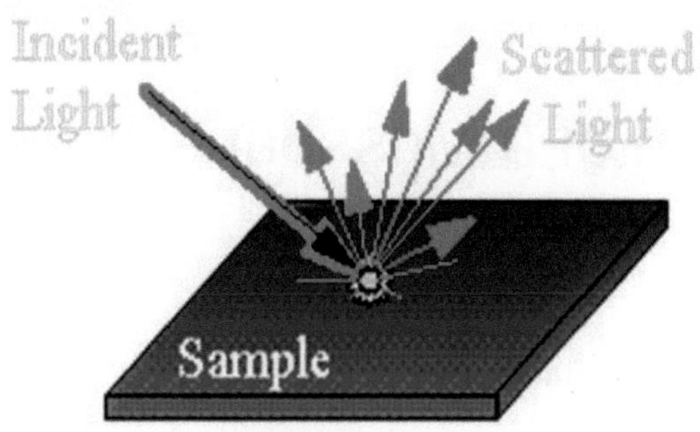

Fig 29 a **Raman Spectroscopy**

It is a light scattering technique,whereby a molecule scatters incident light from a high intensity laser light source.

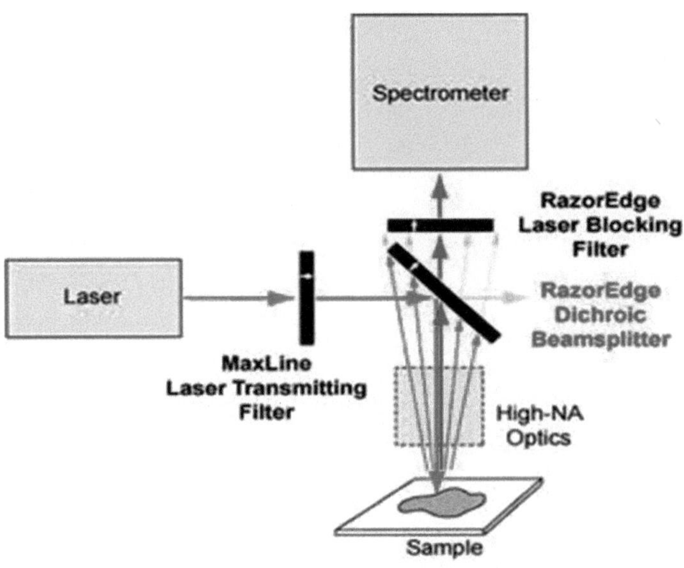

Fig 29 b **Raman Spectroscopy**

4.30 Mossbauer Spectroscopy

- •Special effect, restricted to specific isotopes of certain elements which causes a very characteristic emission (after getting hit with a beam of gamma radiation) which is sensitive to the bonding environment of that isotope (only 57Co, 57Fe, 129I, 119Sn, 121Sb) . Generally used to study Fe – tells us about how Fe is bonded and it's oxidation state.

Instrumentation of a Mossbauer Spectrometer

- Possible arrangements of instrumentation
- Mossbauer Drive
  - Used to move the source relative to sample
- ^{57}Co Source
  - Source of gamma ray emission
- Collimator
  - Used to narrow gamma rays

Mössbauer Drive
Collimator
Detector
^{57}Co Source
Sample
Collimator
Sample
Mössbauer Drive
^{57}Co Source
51

http://serc.carleton.edu/research_education/geochemsheets/techniques/mossbauer.html Detector

Fig 30 **Mossbauer Spectroscopy**

4.30.1 APPLICATIONS:

- It is used to study the structure of atoms and molecules.
- It is also helpful in finding the information of space objects in space.
- It is used in environmental analysis for detecting dissolved oxygen content in water bodies.

4.30.2 Electrical Technique

- Electrical propeerties are a key physical property of conducting materials.
- It is often necessary to accurately measures the resistivity of materials.

4.30.3 Common methods

- Dielectric strength.
- Electrochemical impedence spectroscopy(EIS).
- Arc resistence.
- EMF sheilding test.

4.31 Magnetic technique

- Magnetic method are potential methods for evaluation of surface manifestations such as microstructural degradation residual stresses.

4.31.1 Common Methods :

- Magnetic Adhesive Force Methods:
- It uses the distance dependency of the magnetic
- attractive force between a ferromagnetic substrate
- and a permanent magnet touching the surface of
- Coating, which must be made from a non magnetic
- material. Used to find holding power of magnet
- Magnetically inductive method:
- Another popular method is the magnetically inductive method which is based on measuring the magnetic flux that the passes through a non ferromagnetic coating into a ferromagnetic substrate.

FIVE

THERMAL TESTING AND CHEMICAL TESTING

In this chapter the following testing are explained

·Thermal Testing: Differential scanning calorimetry, Differential thermal analysis.

·Thermo-mechanical and Dynamic mechanical analysis: Principles, Advantages, Applications.

·Chemical Testing: X-Ray Fluorescence

5.1 Thermal Analysis techniques

- When a material is heated its structural and chemical composition can undergo changes such as fusion, melting, crystallization, oxidation, decomposition, transition, expansion and sintering. Using Thermal Analysis such changes can be monitored in every atmosphere of interest. The obtained information is very useful in both quality control and problem solving.

5.1.1 Types of thermal analysis

- Thermogravimetry (TG).
- Differential thermogravimetry (DTG).
- Differential scanning calorimetry (DSC).

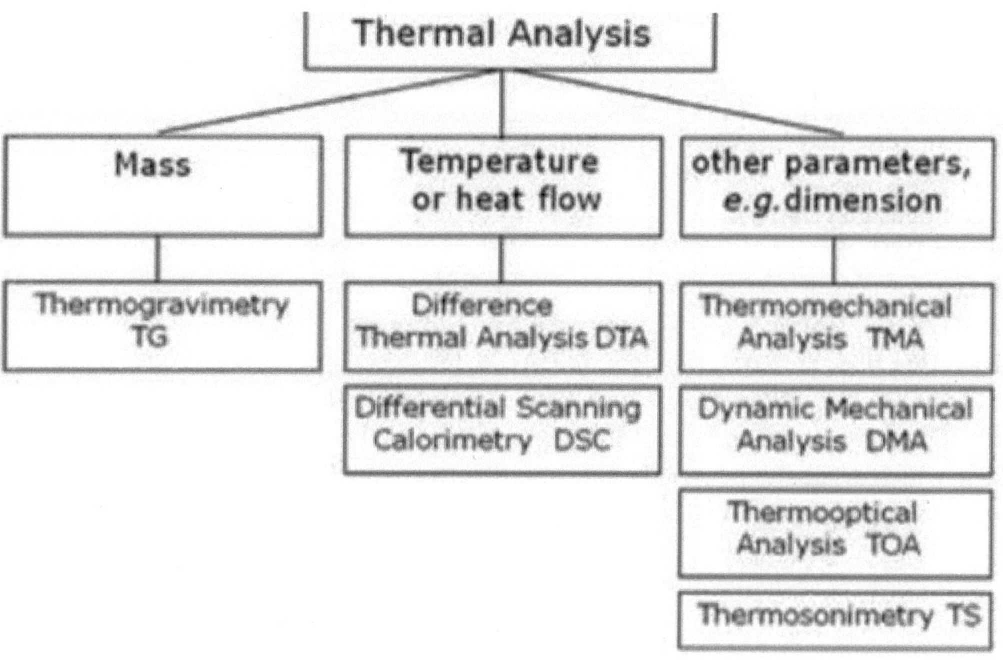

Fig 1 Types of thermal analysis

5.2 Introduction to Differential Scanning calorimetry (DSC)

History of DSC

The technique was developed by E. S. Watson and M. J. O'Neill in 1962, introduced commercially in 1963 at Pittsburgh Conference on Analytical Chemistry and Applied Spectroscopy. First Adiabetic differential scanning calorimeter that could be used in Biochemistry was developed by PL.Privalov in 1964.

5.2.1Differential scanning calorimetry:

Principle:

It is a technique in which the energy necessary to establish a zero temp. difference between the sample & reference material is measured as a function of temp. Here. sample & reference material are heated by separate heaters in such a way that their temp are kept equal while these temp. are increased or decreased linearly

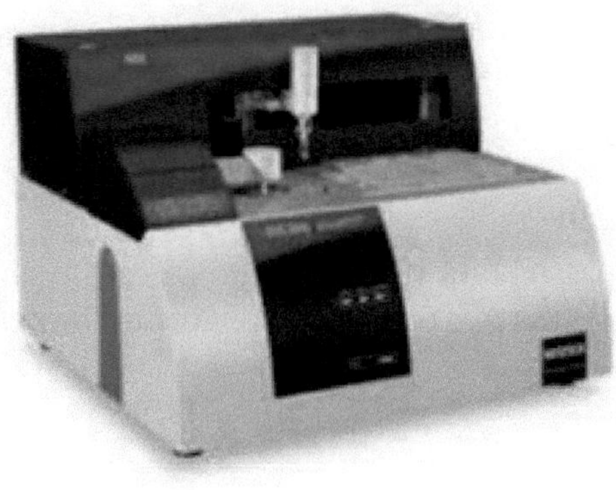

Fig 2 Differential scanning caliometry

DSC Is widely used to measure glass transition temp & characterization of polymer. Glass Transition temp(Tg): Temp at which an amorphous polymer or an amorphous part of crystalline polymer goes from hard brittle state to soft. Rubbery state.

5.2.2 Instrumentation:

There are five different types of DSC instrument:

1. Heat flux DSC
2 Power compensated DSC
3. Modulated DSC
4. Hyper DSC
5. Pressure DSC

5.2.2.1 Heat flux DSC:

In heat flux DSC, the difference in heat flow into the sample and reference is measured while the sample temperature is changed at the constant rate. The main assembly of the DSC cell is enclosed in a cylindrical, silver heating black, which dissipates heat to the specimens via a constantan disc which is attached to the silver block. The disk has two raised platforms on which the sample and reference pans are placed.

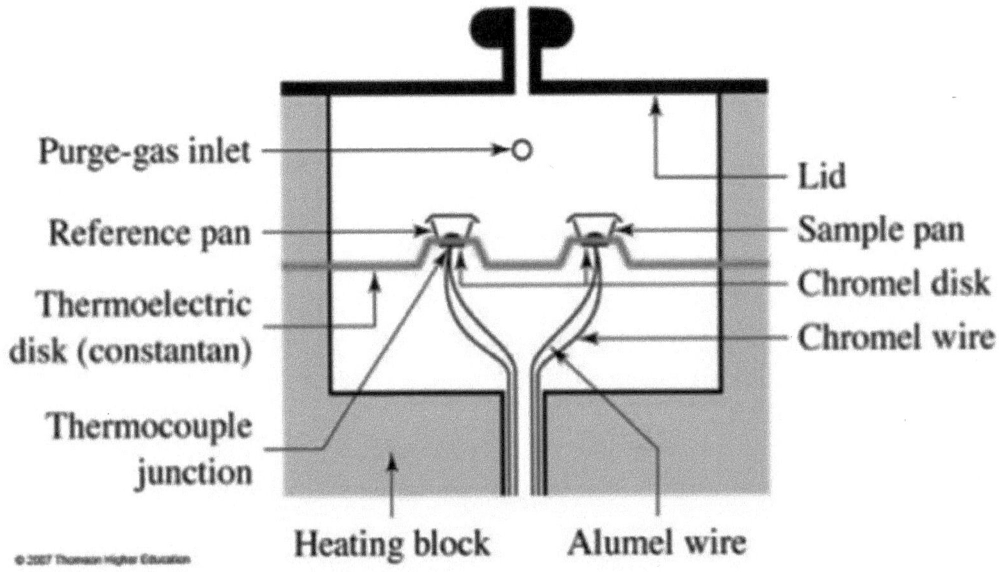

Fig 3 Heat flux DSC

In heat flux DSC, we can write the total heat flow dH/dt as,

dH/dt = Cp dT/dt + f (T,t)

Where, H = enthalpy in J mol-1

Cp-specific heat capacity in JK -1 mol-1

f (T.t)= kinetic response of the sample in J mol-1

Thus, the total heat flow is the sum of the two terms, one related to the heat capacity, and one related to the kinetic response.

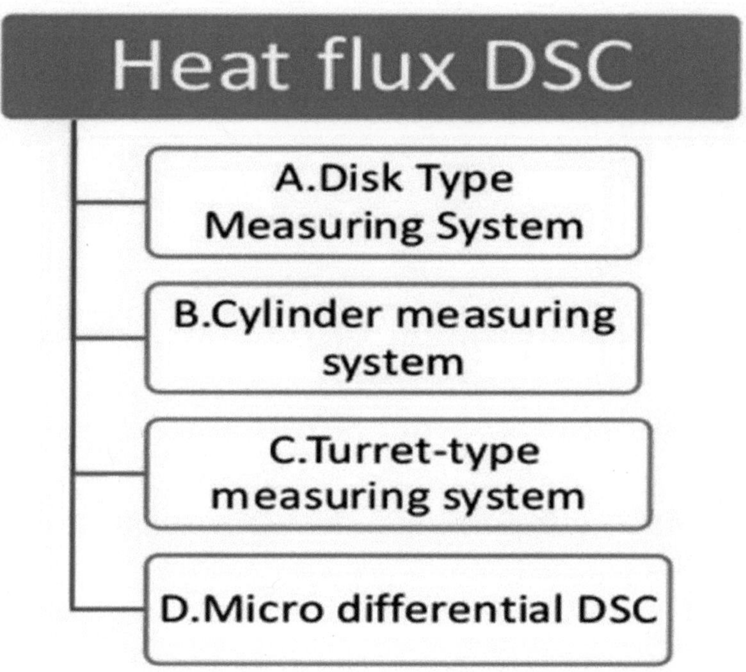

5.2.2.2 Power compensation DSC :

In power compensation DSC, the temperatures of the sample and reference are kept equal to each other while both temperatures are increased or decreased linearly. The power needed to maintain the sample temperature equal to the reference temperature is measured. In power compensation DSC two independent heating units are employed. These heating units are quite small, allowing for rapid rates of heating, cooling and equilibration. The heating units are embedded in a large temperature- controlled heat sink. The sample and reference holders have platinum resistance thermometers to continuously monitor the temperature of the materials. Both sample and reference are maintained at the programmed temperature by applying power to the sample and reference heaters. The instrument records the power difference needed to maintain the sample and reference at the same temperature as a function of the programmed temperatures. Power compensated DSC has lower sensitivity than heat flux DSC, but its response time is more rapid. This makes power compensated DSC well suited for kinetics studies in which fast equilibrations to new temperature settings are needed. it is also capable of higher resolution then heat flux DSC.

All PC DSC are in basic principles the same. But, one of the special PC DSC is photo DSC. Where direct measurements of radiation flow occur under a light source. This way the degradation of material can also be observed. The maximum heating rate for not modified PC DSC is up to 500K/min and the maximum cooling rate is up to 400 K/min. Temperature range of measurement is up to 400 °C with time constant of only 1.5 s or lower. Sample masses are around 20 mg. Crucibles of different volumes (lower than several ten cubic millimeter's) are made mostly of aluminum.

Power compensation DSC :

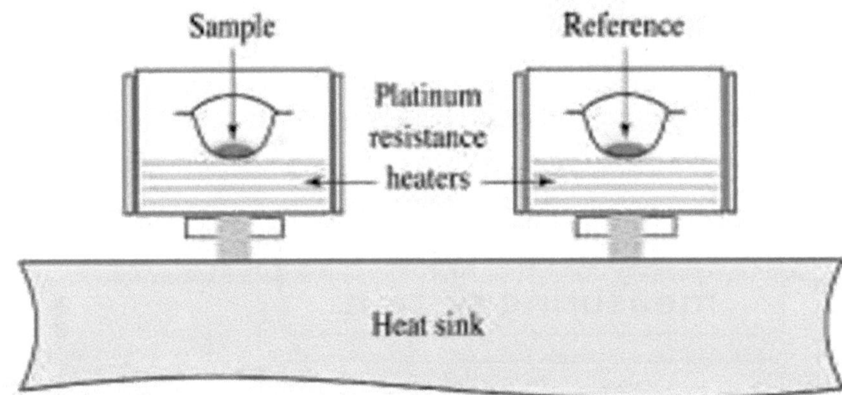

Figure 6: power compensation DSC

34

Fig. 4 Power compensation DSC

5.2.2.3 Modulated DSC

Modulated DSC uses the same heating and cell arrangement as the heat-flux DSC method. it is a new technique introduced in 1993. The main advantage of this technique is the separation of overlapping events in the DSC scans. In MDSC the normally linear heating ramp is overlaid with the sinusoidal function (MDSC) defined by a frequency and amplitude to produce a sine wave shape temperature versus time function. Using Fourier mathematics, the DSC signal is split into two components: reflecting no reversible events (kinetic) and reversible event.

$T\text{-}TO\text{-}bt+B \sin(wt)$

$dq/dt=C\ [b+Bw \cos(wt)] + f(t,T)+K \sin(wt)$

where, T-temperature, C-specific heat, t=time, w=frequency f(t,T)= the average underling kinetic function once the effect of the sine wave modulation has been subtracted.

K= amplitude of the kinetic response to the sine wave modulation.

[b+Bw cos (wt)]=the measured quantity dT/dt or reversing Curve.

MDSC is a valuable extension of conventional DSC. Its applicability is recognized for precise determination of the temperature of glass transition and for the study of the energy of relaxation. It has been applied for the determination of glass transition of Hydroxypropylmethylcellulose films and for the study of amorphous lactose as well as some glassy drugs. The high resolution of PC-DSC or new type of power compensating DSC provides the best results for an analysis of melting and crystallization of metals or detection of glass transition temperature (Tg) in medications. · Fast scan DSC has the ability to perform valid heat flow measurements with fast linear controlled rates (up to 500 K/ min) especially by cooling, where the rates are higher than with the classical PC DSC. Standard DSC operates under 10 K/ min. The benefits of such devices are increased sensitivity at higher rates (which enables a better study of the kinetics in the process), suppression of undesired transformation like solid solid transformation etc. It has a great sensitivity also at a heating rate of 500 K/min with 1 mg of sample material. This technique is especially proper for the pharmaceutics industry for testing medicaments at different temperatures where fast heating rates are necessary to avoid other unwanted reactions etc.

5.2.2.4 Pressure DSC

In pressure DSC, the sample can be submitted to different pressures, which allows the characterization of substances at the pressures of processes or to distinguish between overlapping peaks. Applications of this technique includes studies of pressure sensitive reactions, evaluation of catalysts, and resolution of overlapping transitions.

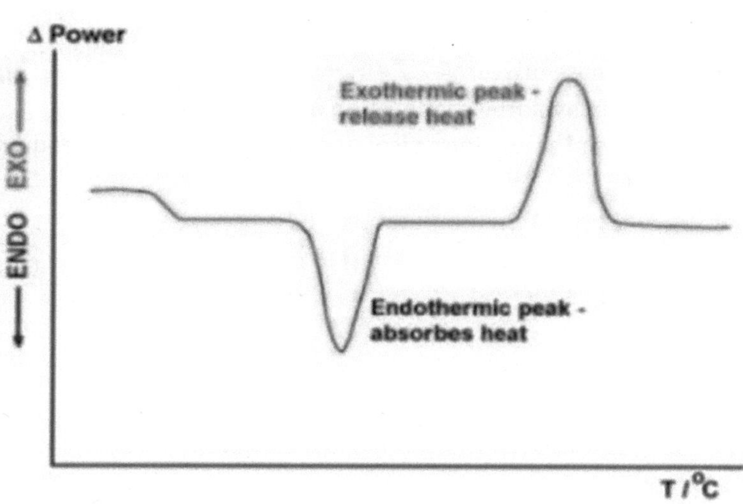

Fig. 5 DSC curve

5.2.3 Typical DSC Curve:

The result of a DSC experiment is a curve of heat flux versus temperature or versus time. There are two different conventions: exothermic reactions in the sample shown with a positive or negative peak, depending on the kind of technology used in the experiment. • This curve can be used to calculate enthalpies of transitions. This is done by integrating the peak corresponding to a given transition. It can be shown that the enthalpy of transition can be expressed using the following equation:

AH= KA

where H is the enthalpy of transition, K is the calorimetric constant, and A is the area under the curve. The calorimetric constant will vary from instrument to instrument, and can be determined by analyzing a well characterized sample with known enthalpies of transition.

5.2.4 Factors Affecting DSC Curve:

Instrumental factors:

- Furnace heating rate
- Recording or chart speed
- Furnace atmosphere
- Geometry of sample holder/location of sensors
- Sensitivity of the recording system
- Composition of sample containers.

5.2.5 Advantages of DSC:

- Instruments can be used at very high temperatures

- Instruments are highly sensitive.
- Flexibility in sample volume/form.
- Characteristic transition or reaction temperatures can be determined.
- High resolution obtained
- High sensitivity
- Stability of the material.

5.2.6 Limitations of DSC:

- DSC generally unsuitable for two-phase mixtures.
- Difficulties in test cell preparation in avoiding evaporation of volatile Solvents.
- DSC is generally only used for thermal screening of isolated intermediates and products.
- Does not detect gas generation.
- Uncertainty of heats of fusion and transition temperatures

5.2.7 Applications:

- Metal alloy melting temperatures and heat of fusion.
- Metal magnetic or structure transition temperatures and heat of transformation.
- Intermetallic phase formation temperatures and exothermal energies.
- Oxidation temperature and oxidation energy.
- Exothermal energy of polymer cure (as in epoxy adhesives), allows determination of the degree and rate of cure.
- Determine the melting behavior of complex organic materials, both temperatures and enthalpies of melting can be used to determine purity of a material.
- Measurement of plastic or glassy material glass transition temperatures or softening temperatures, which change dependent upon the temperature history of the polymer or the amount and type of fill material, among other effects.
- Determines crystalline to amorphous transition temperatures in polymers and plastics and the energy associated with the transition.
- Crystallization and melting temperatures and phase transition energies for inorganic compounds.
- Oxidative induction period of an oil or fat.
- My be used as one of multiple techniques to identify an unknown material or by itself to confirm that it is the expected material.
- Determine the thermal stability of a material.
- Determine the reaction kinetics of a material.
- Measure the latent heat of melting of nylon 6 in a nylon Spandex fabric to determine the weight percentage of the nylon

5.3 Differential thermal analysis

Differential thermal analysis is also known as thermography. The measurement of change in heat content is carried out by heating the two materials at elevated temperature or cooling to subnormal temperature at a predetermined rate.

5.3.1. Principle of working

The thermal effect associated with the physical and chemical changes are measured by a differential method in which the sample temperature is continuously compared against the temperature of thermally inert material. The differential temperature, AT is recorded as a function of reference material temperature or time, assuming that the furnace temperature rise is linear with time.

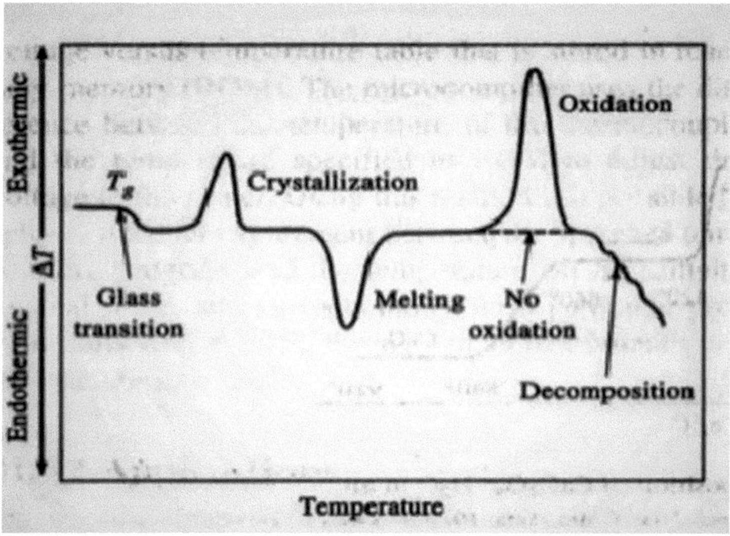

FIg. 6 DTA Curve

The thermal effects may be either endothermic or exothermic. Enthalpic changes are caused by physical phenomina such as fusion, crystalline structure invertion, boiling, vapourisation, sublimation, and others. Some enthalpic changes are also caused by chemical reactions like decomposition, oxidation, dehydration, reduction, compination, displacement etc. The endo or exothermic bands and peaks appearing on the thermogram give information regarding the detection of enthalpic changes.

5.3.2 Factors affecting the DTA Curve

- Instrumental Factors:
- Size and shape of the sample and furnace holder.
- Material from which sample holder is made and its corrosive attack.
- Heating rate(furnace heating rate)
- Sample characteristics:
- Amount of the sample(sample weight)
- Particle size of the sample

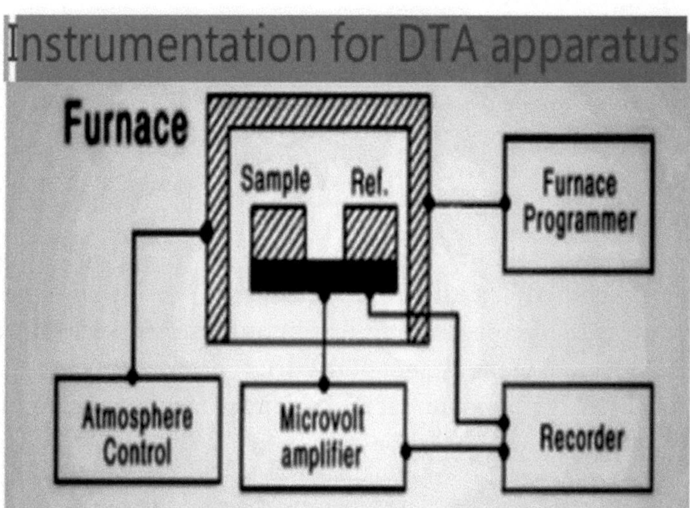

Fig.7 DTA Instruments

5.3.4 Furnace: Device for heating the sample. ii. Sample holder: Used to contain the sample as well as the referece materials.

DC Amplifier: Genarally a low level DC amplifier is employed.

Differential temperature detector: It measures the differential temperatue.

Furnace temperature programmer: Used to increase the temperature of fumace at a steady rate.

Recorder: This is to record the DTA curve.

Control equipment: Maintains a suitable atmosphere in the fuenace and sample holder.

Furnace

- Device for heating the sample. In DTA apparatus, tubular furnace is prefered. Constructed by appropriate material (wire or ribbon) wound on a refractory tube. It possess desired characteristics for good temperature regulation and programming. The choice of the resistant material and that of refractory is decided from the intended maximum temperatures of operation and gaseous environment. The dimension depends up on the length of the uniform temperature zone desired. The size of the sample holder, heating rate and cost are also

Sample Holders

It used to contain the sample as well as the reference material.

Material

Both metalic and non-metalic materials are used for the fabrication of sample holder.

Metalic materials genarally include nickel, stainless steal, platinum and its alloys.

Metalic holders give rise to sharp exotherms and flat endotherms.

Non-metalic matrials include glass, viterous silica or sintered alumina.

- --give rise to sharp endotherms and flat

5.3.5 Temperature controller and recorder

- Temperature control
- The basic elements required are sensor, control element and heater
- Control element governs the rate of heat input required to match the heat loss from the system.
- The two methods for controlling temperature:
- --On-off control: If the sensor-signal indicates that the temperature has become greater than the point, the heater is immediately cut off
- --Proportional control: The heat input to the system progressively reduced as the temperature aprroaches the desired value.

5.3.6 Temperature programming

- It transmits certain time-based instruction to the control unit.
- The simplest device is to use a variable speed motor-driven autotransformer which gives a power input to the furnace that is proportional to the rate of movement of the drive mechanism.
- It can archive the linear rate of heating or cooling if the autotransformer is driven in a non linear fation using a special cam-drive.

5.3.7 Thermocouples

- They are the temperature sensors in most of the DTA and TG instruments.
- The voltage signal produced between the two hetero-juntions of the thermocouple depends up on the temperature difference between these two junctions.
- The following points has to be considered while selecting the thermocouples as the temperature sensor:Temperature interval, Thermoelectric coefficient, Chemical compactibility with the sample, availability and cost, chemical gaseous environment used and reproducibility of the EMF vs Temperature curve as a function of thermal cycling.

5.3.8 Cooling device

- The cooling system is cosidered separate from the temperature programmer because in most instruments cooling is completely independant of heating.

5.3.9 Advantages:

- Instruments can be used at a very high temperature
- Instruments are highly sensitive
- Flexibility in crucible volume/form
- Characteristic transition or reaction temperature can be accurately determined

5.3.10 Disadvantages:

- Reaction or transition estimations is only 20% to 50% DTA
- Uncertainty in heats of fusion

5.3.11 Applications of DTA

- Determination of heat of reaction
- Determination of specific heat of substane
- Determination of thermal diffusivity
- Identification of substances
- Identification of the products
- Determination of melting point
- Quantitative analysis
- Quality control

5.4 THERMO-MECHANICAL ANALYSIS

A technique in which a deformation of the sample under non-oscillating stress is monitored against time or temperature while the temperature the sample, in a specified atmosphere, is programmed. Thermo mechanical analysis (TMA) easily and rapidly measures sample displacement (growth, shrinkage, movement, etc.) as a function of temperature, time and applied force.

5.4.1 PRINCIPLE

Thermo mechanical analysis (TMA) is used to measure the dimensional changes of a material as a function of temperature by applying stress. The stress may be compression, tension, flexure or torsion.

5.4.2 COMPONENTS

- Transducer (Linear Variable Displacement Transducer (LVDT), laser optoelectronic etc.,
- Probe (made up of quartz glass)

- Thermocouple Furnace
- Force generator

5.4.3 CONSTRUCTION AND WORKING

The sample is inserted into the furnace and is touched by the probe which is connected with the Length Detector and the Force Generator. The construction of the pushrod and sample holder depends on the mode of the measurements. The thermocouple for temperature measurement is located next sample. The rate of 5° C/min is usually the maximum recommended value for good temperature equilibration across the specimen The sample temperature is changed in the furnace by applying the fore onto the the Force Generator via probe.

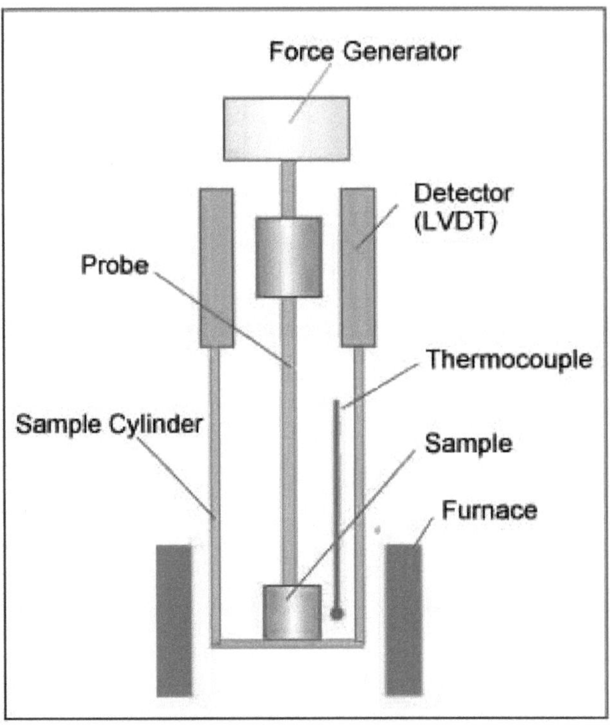

Fig 8 THERMO-MECHANICAL ANALYSIS

The sample deformation such as Thermal Expansion and Softening wih changing temperature is measured as the probe displacement by Length Detector. Linear Variable Differential Transformer (LVDT) is used for Length Detection sensor. Every displacement of the pushrod is trans-formed into an analog signal by the LVDT, converted to digital form and then recorded in the computer system, and finally presented by the software as a dimensional change versus time or temperature.

5.4.4 APPLICATION

- Measurement of Dimensional Change
- Coefficient of Linear Thermal Expansion
- Determination of Material Anisotropy

5.5 THERMO MECHANICAL DYNAMIC ANALYSIS

Thermo mechanical dynamic analysis, otherwise known as Dynamic Mechanical Analysis (DMA), is a technique where a small deformation is applied to a sample in a cyclic manner. This allows the materials response to stress, temperature, frequency and other values to be studied. The term is also used to refer to the analyzer that performs the test. Dynamic mechanical analysis (DMA) is an important technique used to measure the mechanical and viscoelastic properties of materials such as thermoplastics, thermosets, elastomers, ceramics and metals.

5.5.1 PRINCIPLE

A sinusoidal stress is applied and the strain in the material is measured, allowing one to determine the complex modulus. The temperature of the sample or the frequency of the stress are often varied, leading to variations in the complex modulus; this approach can be used to locate the temperature of the material, as well as to identify transitions corresponding to other molecular motions.

5.5.2 TYPES OF THERMO MECHANICAL DYNAMIC ANALYZER

Forced resonance analyzers - Analyzers force the sample to oscillate at a certain frequency and are reliable for performing a temperature sweep. Free resonance analyzers- Free resonance analyzers measure the free oscillations of damping of the sample being tested by suspending and swinging the sample

5.5.3 MODE OF ANALYZER

Stress (force) control - The structure of the sample is less likely to be destroyed and longer relaxation times/ longer creep studies can be done. Strain (displacement) control-The better short time response for materials of low viscosity and experiments of stress relaxation are done with relative ease

5.5.4 COMPONENTS

Transducer Sensor (Linear Variable Displacement Transducer (LVDT)-It is which measures a change in voltage. Drive shaft or probe - It is a support and guidance system to act as a guide for the force from the motor to the sample Drive motor - A linear motor for probe loading which provides load for the applied force. Stepper motor-It controls the specimen dimension and measurement

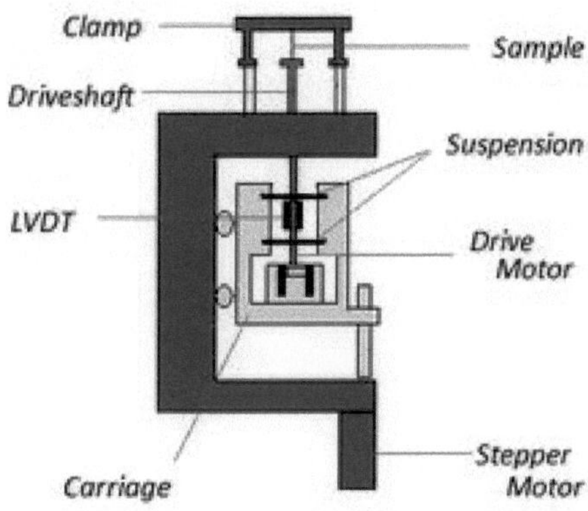

Fig 9 THERMO MECHANICAL DYNAMIC ANALYSIS

5.5.5 WORKING

The sample is clamped in the measurement head of the DMA instrument. During measurement, sinusoidal force is applied to the sample via the probe or driving shaft. Deformation caused by the sinusoidal force is detected and the relation between the deformation and the applied force is measured. Properties such as elasticity and viscosity are calculated from the applied stress and strain plotted as a function of temperature or time.

5.5.6 DIFFERENT LOADING MODES

The most suitable type should be selected depending on the sample shape. modulus and measurement purpose.

5.5.7 ADVANTAGES

- It is an essential analytical technique to determining the viscoelastic properties of polymers.
- Very soft and hard samples are measured.
- Allows accurate temperature measurement.
- It can provide major and minor transitions of materials
- It is also more sensitive.

- It is able to quickly scan and calculate the modulus for a range of temperatures.
- It is the only technique that can determine the basic structure of a polymer system
- This analytical method is able to accurately predict the performance of materials in use.

5.5.8 LIMITATIONS

- It leads to calculation inaccuracies.
- The large inaccuracies are introduced if dimensional measurements of samples are slightly inaccurate.
- The oscillating stress converts mechanical energy to heat and changes the temperature of the sample.
- The maintaining an exact temperature is important in temperature scans, this also introduces inaccuracies.
- The final source of measurement uncertainty comes from computer error.

5.5.9 DMA MEASURES

- Displacement and force
- Wide range of force ImN to 40N
- Wide range of frequency 0.001 to 1000Hz.
- Wide stiffness range.

5.5.10 APPLICATION

- Measurement of the glass transition temperature of polymers
- Varying the composition of monomers Effectively evaluate the miscibility of polymers
- To characterize the glass transition temperature of a material.
- Mechanical properties in the relevant frequency range
- Modulus information
- Measurement of different relaxations
- Molecular interaction
- Nonlinear properties
- Damping behaviour

5.6 CHEMICAL TESTING

Chemical Testing provides a variety of quantitative and qualitative services for verification, identification and component analysis of ferrous and non-ferrous metals.

5.6.1 PURPOSE OF CHEMICAL TESTING

- Chemical Trace Analysis
- Elemental Trace Analysis
- Failure Analysis
- Contamination Analysis
- Materials Analysis and Testing
- Material Verification
- Material Identification
- Chemical Composition Analysis

5.6.2 CHEMICAL COMPOSITION TECHNIQUE AND TESTS

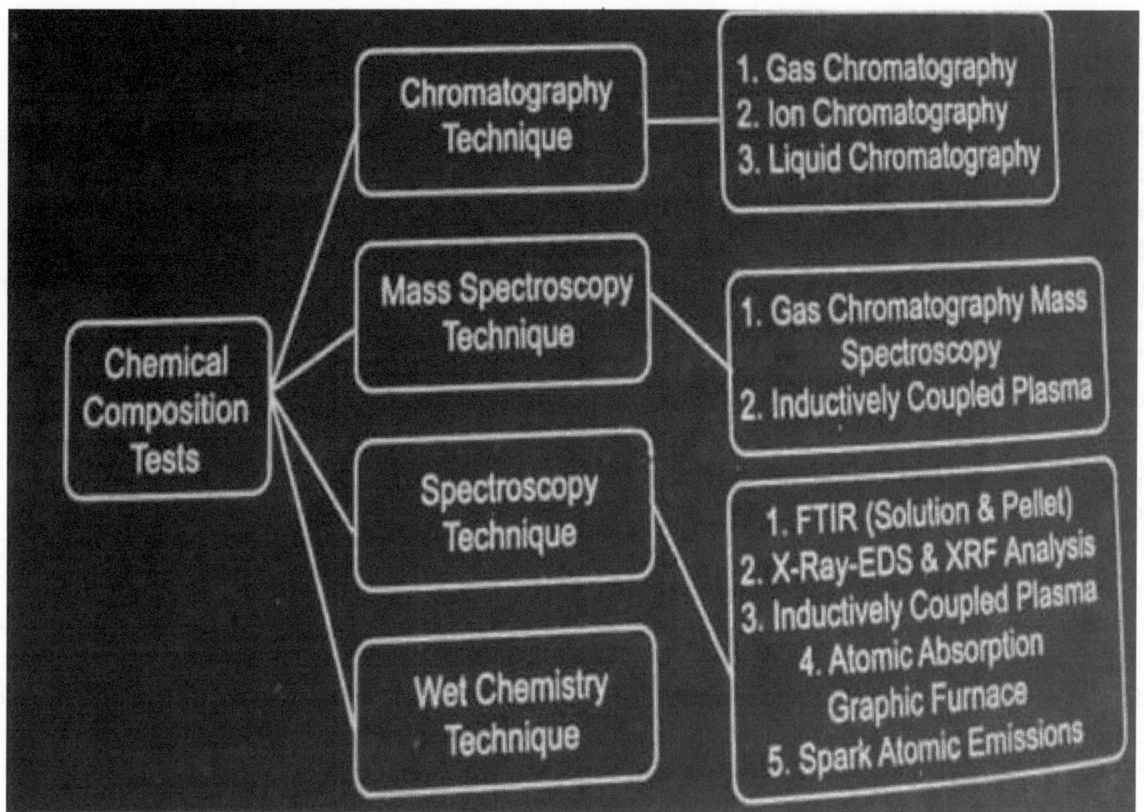

(a) Chromatography Technique

- Gas Chromatography
- Ion Chromatography
- Liquid Chromatography

(b) Mass Spectroscopy Technique

- Gas Chromatography Mass Spectroscopy
- Inductively Coupled Plasma

(c) Spectroscopy Technique

- Fourier-transform infrared spectroscopy (Solution & Pellet)
- X-Ray - EDS & XRF Analysis
- Inductively Coupled Plasma (ICP-AES)
- Atomic Absorption Graphite Furnace (GF-AAS)
- Spark Atomic Emissions (Spark-AES)

(d) Wet chemistry technique

5.6.1 X-RAY FLUORESCENCE

XRF (X-ray fluorescence) is a non-destructive analytical technique used to determine the elemental composition of materials. XRF analyzers determine the chemistry of a sample by measuring the fluorescent X-ray emitted from a sample when it is excited by a primary X-ray source. The phenomenon is widely used for elemental analysis and chemical analysis, particularly in the investigation of metals, glass, ceramics and building materials, and for research in geochemistry.

5.6.2 PRINCIPLE

X-ray fluorescence (XRF) is the emission of characteristic "secondary" fluorescent) X-rays from a material that has been excited by being bombarded with high-energy X-rays or gamma rays.

5.6.3 COMPONENTS OF A TYPICAL XRF SPECTROMETER

Source of X-rays used irradiate the sample. Wavelengths are typically in the range 0.01 to 10 nm, which is equivalent to energies of 125 keV to 0.125 keV. Detection equipped by Gas-filled detectors, semiconductor detector, scintillation detector, a photographic plate.

5.6.4 TYPES OF XRF SPECTROSCOPY.

The XRF spectroscopy differs primarily by detection and analyzing.

- Energy Dispersive XRF (Direct and polarized excitation)
- Wavelength Dispersive XRF

5.6.5 WORKING OF X-RAY FLUORESCENCE

A solid or a liquid sample is irradiated with high energy X-rays from controlled X-ray tube. When an atom in the sample is struck with an X-ray of sufficient an electron from one of the atorn's inner orbital shells is removed. energy The atom regains stability, filling the vacancy left in the inner orbital shell with an electron from one of the atom's higher energy orbital shells. The electron drops to the lower energy state by releasing a fluorescent X-ray. The energy of this X-ray is equal to the specific difference in energy between two quantum states of the electron. The measurement of this energy is the basis of XRF analysis. The intensity of each characteristic radiation is directly related to the amount of each element in the material.

5.6.6 APPLICATIONS

- It is a method of elemental (metal and Nonmetal) analysis with atomi number greater than 12.
- Quantitative analysis can be carried out by measuring the intensity of fluorescence at the wavelength characteristics of the element being determined, especially applicable to most of the element in the period table.
- Research in igneous, sedimentary, and metamorphic petrology, Sa surveys, Mining (e.g., measuring the grade of ore),Cement production Ceramic and glass manufacturing
- Metallurgy (e.g., quality control)
- Environmental studies (e.g., analyses of particulate matter on air filter)
- Petroleum industry (e.g., sulfur content of crude oils and petroleum products)
- Field analysis in geological and environmental studies (using portable hand-held XRF spectrometers)
- Bulk chemical analyses of major elements and trace elements

5.6.7 ADVANTAGES

- Simple spectra analysis
- XRF is a versatile and rapid technique
- Easily analysis of the element among the same family elements
- It is non-destructive method of chemical analysis
- Important as in case of samples in limited amounts, or valuable or irreplaceable
- It is precise and with skilled operations it is accurate
- Applicable to a wide variety of samples from powders to liquids
- It is convenient and economical to use

- The instruments have few moving parts, tend to be low-maintenance, and on a regular basis consume only liquid nitrogen and electricity Spectral positions are almost independent of the chemical state of the analyses
- Applicable over a wide range of concentrations

5.6.8 DISADVANTAGES

- It fairly high limits of detection when compared to other methods
- Possibility of matrix effects, although these can usually be accounted for using software-based correction procedures
- It is limited in their ability to precisely and accurately measure the abundances of elements with Atomic number <11 in most natural earb materials
- XRF analyses cannot distinguish variations among isotopes of an element XRF analyses cannot distinguish ions of the same element in different valence states
- Instrumentation is fairly expensive

Printed by Libri Plureos GmbH in Hamburg,
Germany